Dare to Live the Truth You Believe

LAURA ROSS GREINER

Kregel
Publications

Library of Congress Cataloging-in-Publication Data
Greiner, Laura Ross
TruthDare : dare to live the truth you believe / Laura Ross Greiner.
    p. cm.
1. Christian women—Religious life. I. Title. II. Title: Truth dare.
BV4527.G7418   2010   248.8'43—dc22   2010000714

ISBN 978-0-8254-2738-1

Thank you to the men and women who opened their lives and shared their stories for this book. I pray that as their stories bless readers, they in turn will be richly blessed!

Thank you to my supportive family: my kids, Travis, Jenna, and AJ, who are always interested in my work and ask great questions about it; and my husband, Bruce, who is my best friend and partner as we journey together to live the Truth we deeply believe.

Contents

Contents

Introduction

Truth . . . and Dare

I went out to dinner this weekend with a close friend whose life is so full of pain, it nauseates me at times. She has an eleven-year-old daughter who was born with brain abnormalities and will never function past the capabilities of a six-month-old baby. This requires my friend to be a 24-7 caregiver, which, needless to say, is emotionally and physically exhausting. She also has a teenage son who struggles with depression, and suicide is a real and ongoing concern for this boy. If this wasn't enough, she has three brothers who sold their late father's company a few years ago and, consumed by greed and self-justifications, managed to exclude her from their family's inheritance.

This is what my friend wakes up to every morning. But guess what my friend did when we were out for dinner? She knew I was having a rough bout with my own hormonal teenage son, so she bought me a gift and paid for the meal. Never mind that the pain in her life renders her to a heap on the bathroom floor. Never mind that worry over her son keeps her from getting a full night of sleep. My friend's heart aches much of the time. Yet she took me out to dinner and bought me a present.

My friend—in spite of the odds and injustices stacked against her—embraces the truth of God and dares to live it. Not that she doesn't have it out with God on occasion, because she does. But at the end of the day her pain and questions don't trump her faith. *TruthDare* is filled with men and women like my friend—people who have taken God at His word in spite of their circumstances, questions, feelings, and fears. This book is also born out of a hunger deep inside my soul. Most of my life I've wanted more of God. I've craved a deeper, mountain-moving faith, yet I never seem to get where I yearn to be. I want all of God that my humanness can take—an abandoned Jesus-centered life, trusting Him with every detail and knowing myself as His beloved.

But how?

One way I've found to inch toward this place is through God's stories. When I was a child, I was given a collection of books on martyrs and strong people of faith. I remember reading their stories and even as a little girl having the flame of my own faith fueled. I'm an avid believer in the faith-breathing impact of real-life stories that tell about the messy stuff in life. I think they take us "farther up and further in" to God, as C. S. Lewis put it in *The Last Battle*.

My friend Carol trains women at her church how to share their stories. In her training, she describes how stories have the power to make God and faith more real to us. As a college psychology teacher, I share with my students how our brains are wired to retain and remember information we can emotionally connect with. It's no wonder then that God is an avid storyteller. Jesus used stories to illustrate His teachings because He wanted us to connect with and remember what He taught us. And God's stories don't end with the Scriptures but are timeless and pervasive, continuously being told all around us.

Inside this book you'll find people who unknowingly have moved me closer to God by sharing from their own barren, disappointed, and confused places. Their stories are also filled with grace, triumph, and celebration. These men and women have grappled with everyday messes as well as life-altering events and found their way closer to God. Coming to Him with humble and hungry hearts, they have uncovered and rejected lies in their lives and have sought to listen to the One whose voice inspires them to dare to live His Word.

As I grow closer to God, I see myself as a tiny inchworm crossing the desert, and these stories nourish me on my long, slow journey. So in each chapter I weave in pieces of my own story, sharing personal struggles and discoveries as my heart hungers to live this *TruthDare*.

1

Remember

God is real. See the proof.

Do this to remember me.

LUKE 22:19 (NLT)

In the nearly thirty years I've believed that Jesus is who He said He is, I've passed through many hallways of doubt. I've asked all the same questions I'm now asked as a neighborhood Bible study leader. Many times I have no answers for the questions I'm asked. And the truth is, at this point in my spiritual journey, I'm scared of people who seem to have all the answers. Clean, logical, cut-and-dried answers often make me uncomfortable. One woman in our study had memorized practically the whole Bible, and whenever someone asked a vulnerable question such as, "Why would God allow my sister's baby to born deformed?" this woman would pull out some verse from the Bible about trust, or God's goodness, or the sanctification process. She meant well but I always cringed when she gave her answers.

For me a lot of real life doesn't make sense or have a simplistic spiritual answer. Besides, as far as I can tell, almost every person chosen

by God in the Bible to lead others had questions, doubts, and a need for reassurance. I want to fall into the same category as them. Not the Bible Answer Man.

Jesus' disciple Thomas is known as "the doubter," but I've always wondered how John the Baptist—whom Jesus called the greatest man who ever lived—scooted through history, never being dubbed a doubter. He spent his whole life following the call God had given him—to prepare the way for the Messiah. Then, when Jesus came to John while he was baptizing people in the river, John saw "the Spirit of God descending like a dove" onto Jesus, and he heard a voice from heaven say, "This is my Son, whom I love" (Matt. 3:16–17). After John saw and heard this spectacular event, he told anyone who would listen that Jesus was THE ONE—the Messiah who would save them.

> He said to his disciples, "Why are you so afraid?
> Do you still have no faith?"
> MARK 4:40

Yet, when John was thrown into prison a short time later, he began to have doubts. What he had seen and heard by the river became blurred. John wanted reassurance so he sent friends to go to Jesus and double-check with him. "Are you actually THE ONE?" Just sort of a last ditch, double-triple check. I love what Jesus tells John's friends: "Tell him what you have seen and heard" (see Luke 7:22). Basically, Jesus was jogging John's memory: "John, remember. Remember what you saw and heard. Remember what happened by the river . . . you can't see it now but it's still real . . . it's true . . . remember."

I relate to John in his moment of crisis because I'm prone to forgetting. And when I forget, my thoughts can go dark too. I start wondering why God allows mothers to die while their children are still young. That kills me. I wonder about how He can stand to watch a little girl go hungry. I wonder about the little children who drowned when He flooded the earth. I volunteer at our local hospice and I watch people in horrific agony as they die, and I wonder, "Why God? Why does it have to be so awful?"

My good friend Ray, who is a theologian, explains these unexplainable things to his students using an analogy he calls the "Thin Man." On a napkin he draws a stick figure and holds it up. "The Thin Man is only two-dimensional," he explains. "He can see only from his limited two-dimensional world. But what if he were able to step out of the napkin and step into our three-dimensional world? He'd be able to see things he never knew were there. Mr. Thin Man would perceive and understand so much more if he were able to become three-dimensional."

His point is that we are like Mr. Thin Man. We're stuck. We're only three-dimensional. There's so much reality beyond our realm that we can't see, understand, or comprehend.

According to Ray's friend Dave, who is a brilliant physicist, when time and space were created, the universe shrunk from seven dimensions to three dimensions. What would life be like in seven dimensions? When I think of it this way, 1 Corinthians 2:9 is given a lot more meaning: "No eye has seen, no ear has heard, no mind has conceived what God has prepared for those who love him."

But even though the Mr. Thin Man analogy makes sense, the fact is we still exist in this pain-saturated, three-dimensional space. The older I get, the more acutely I'm aware of the multitude of hurting people all around me. Sometimes when I'm thinking dark thoughts, I wonder when my time for soul-wrenching pain will come. Is it just around the corner? Is my daughter's headache a brain tumor?

When I go dark like John in prison, I begin questioning if what I believe is really real. When talking to someone doesn't help and my heart is so broken about a friend's marriage hitting rock bottom or an atrocity that just happened in the world, I retreat downstairs and sit

on the couch where I spend my mornings with God. Somehow, if I force myself to bare my heartache and doubts and questions to Him, He meets me. I mostly don't get answers but I do get balm. Soothing, healing balm over my unsteady heart. And often the balm is a gentle reminder to remember.

When I begin to remember, my thoughts slowly shift from dark and questioning to Jesus by the river. But my river experience isn't a dove or a voice from above. It's a six-year-old boy named Oliver.

. . . .

"My tummy hurts." Three-year-old Oliver held his stomach and looked up at his parents, Molly and Tom, with tears rolling down his face.

At first Molly hadn't been concerned about Oliver's stomachache, but now as she looked at her son's face, she knew something was wrong.

Molly and Tom prayed as they drove Oliver to the emergency room. At the hospital, a young doctor examined Oliver, looking down his throat and into his ears and poking and prodding all around his abdomen. Looping his stethoscope around his neck, the doctor patted Oliver's shoulder. "He's constipated. Go home and feed him lots of fiber and he'll be better in a couple of days." Relieved, Molly and Tom stopped by the grocery store on the way home and loaded up on Metamucil wafers and mineral oil.

But the constipation remedies didn't work. When they took Oliver back to the doctor's office, they were instructed to give him enemas to help with his discomfort. But still little Oliver kept crying day after day with pain. Finally, after six weeks and every constipation remedy they could discover, Molly and Tom were back in the emergency room for the third time.

"We're not leaving here until the doctors figure out what's wrong,"

Tom told their emergency room nurse, Ursula. His face was drawn tight as he held Oliver's little hand.

After Ursula gave Oliver two enemas herself and had no success, she agreed something more had to be done. The doctors ordered blood tests and an ultrasound and had Oliver admitted to the hospital for further testing.

Molly and Tom helped Oliver get settled in his room and were thankful when a nurse brought in *The Little Mermaid* movie, which distracted Oliver for the moment. When the phone rang later that afternoon, Molly leaned over in her chair next to Oliver's bed and answered it. "Hello."

Tom watched Molly from a chair on the other side of Oliver's bed.

"Yes . . . Uh-huh." Molly nodded. "Oh," her voice went flat. "Okay . . . "

"What is he saying? What?" Tom tried to whisper but it came out more like a shout vibrating off the white, sterile walls.

Molly held up her hand, motioning him to wait, but he pushed ahead. "What is he telling you?"

Molly slowly set down the phone. Bewildered, she looked at Tom. "He was telling me Oliver has cancer."

Time stopped. The room grew small as they both looked down at Oliver curled up in the hospital bed. *Cancer? Oliver? No. That can't be.*

Thirty minutes later Tom and Molly sat at a long rectangular table in a hospital meeting room with pediatric oncologists and both sets of their parents. Molly sat on one side of the table with her mom and dad, and Tom sat on the other side of the table with his mom and dad. The head physician of the pediatric cancer department calmly read the test results to them and explained that Oliver had neuroblastoma, a rare form of childhood cancer with a low survival rate. Molly and Tom locked eyes across the table as the doctor reviewed the results. The unspoken emotions of their nightmare settled over the room like a dark cloud.

The doctor explained there was a mass on Oliver's adrenal gland, and the cancer had already spread extensively throughout his small, thirty-three-pound body. He explained how they would fight it. He made it clear it would be a long, horrendous, uphill battle that needed to begin immediately.

Two days later Oliver had surgery to remove the cancerous mass. The following day he began chemotherapy. The intrusive procedures were unending for Oliver. Most of the really painful procedures took place in the hospital's infamous fourth-floor Treatment Room. The sterile, windowless room had a single stainless steel bed surrounded by tubes, syringes, straps, and monitors. Each time Oliver had a bone aspiration, he would walk bravely through the double white doors into the Treatment Room and crawl up onto the uninviting bed. Molly or Tom would get up on the bed too and lay down with him. Oliver would roll over on his side and press his nose against the nose of one of his parents while technicians drove the five-inch needle into the small of his back. As they lie there, facing each other nose-to-nose, Oliver's big brown eyes would pierce into the eyes of his mom or dad, drinking in the strength he needed to get through it.

After weeks of chemotherapy, it was time for the bone-marrow transplant. Oliver flew to California with his parents to begin a grueling three-month treatment. Molly and Tom lived at the Ronald McDonald House for families while Oliver resided in a highly sterilized, positive airflow room in the Los Angles Children's Hospital. To enter Oliver's special room, Molly and Tom would step into a square "sterile zone" and pull on a sterilized plastic suit that zipped up from the inside. Next, they put on two sets of gloves and finally a full face and head covering so only their eyes were showing. Oliver had little physical contact with anyone during this time, including the nurses who took care of him by using special arm inserts that went through the wall into his room. For more than six weeks, Molly and Tom could not touch or kiss their very sick little boy.

Finally, the day came when Oliver's blood count was up to seven hundred, the magical number allowing physical contact with him. Molly burst into Oliver's room, stripped him down to his diaper, and softly touched his skin all over. Tummy, back, legs, arms—she drank him up with her hands while Oliver rolled all around and giggled.

With each day Oliver grew stronger, and after twelve agonizing weeks the doctors released him to go home. Life slowly resumed to normal. Oliver's hair grew back, and in the fall he started kindergarten. He loved cowboys and fire trucks and fought with his little brother and sister. Life was good again.

One October evening a year and a half later, while Tom was out of town, Molly took the kids to McDonald's to play and eat dinner. The next morning she noticed Oliver was limping. *He must have hurt himself in the ball pit,* she thought while scrambling eggs for the children. When she mentioned his limp to her mom on the phone, they both dismissed it as nothing. Later that afternoon a spasm of panic shot through Molly as she watched her firstborn son shuffle across the kitchen favoring one leg. *The cancer is back.* She stood frozen, her eyes glued to Oliver. When he looked over at her, she forced a smile.

"I'm gonna go call Daddy," she said, injecting a false cheerful note into her voice. In her bedroom she sank onto the bed, a burning sensation filling her chest like a balloon. She tried Tom's number but there was no answer. Crushing loneliness poured over her. If the cancer was back, there were no more medical options for Oliver. "Tom," she whispered, clutching her face in her hands, "call home." A thick fog enveloped her as she walked into the bathroom and locked the door. There, she fell to her knees as sob after sob rose up from her throat. *No. Please, God. No.*

A few weeks later, tests confirmed what they already knew in their hearts. Oliver only had a short time left to live.

Even though grief consumed their hearts, Molly and Tom were

resolved to live big while Oliver was still alive. They went to Disney World, drove around their city in a real fire truck, flew in a twin-engine airplane, and spent lazy days just being together at their country farm. Oliver slept nestled between Molly and Tom every night. He woke up when his brothers and sister climbed into the bed, begging for breakfast. And, although he was often in pain, he always let his new baby brother, Patrick, crawl all over him.

The doctors and specialists advised Molly and Tom not to talk about dying until Oliver brought it up. They suggested it was best to follow his lead. They also suggested Molly and Tom have a plan for what they wanted to do when the end came. Did they want to be alone or with family? Did they want their other children present or at a neighbor's house? As much as they yearned for a miracle, Molly and Tom heeded this advice and talked through these questions.

Gradually, Oliver began to weaken and the pain intensified. He began to use his morphine pump continuously, which caused him to sleep day and night. A nurse came to their house every morning to monitor Oliver's pulse and breathing. She explained that as his body shut down, his vision would go too. A few short weeks after Oliver celebrated his sixth birthday, the nurse came in the morning as usual to check his vital signs. Turning to Molly and Tom, she hesitated for a moment, and then spoke: "It will happen today. He will die within the next several hours."

Molly walked to the phone and began to call their family. Always surrounded by lots of people, Molly and Tom had more than thirty of their family and friends sitting in their living room that day while Oliver lay on their couch. Molly sat on the couch holding Oliver in her arms, while Tom sat to the side, stroking his little boy's hair. Oliver still had never talked to his mom or dad about dying and, during the past week, he'd hardly moved or spoken at all. But that afternoon, all of a sudden, his big brown eyes opened and he began talking. At first he began chatting about cowboys, one of his favorite topics. The whole room smiled as he talked. Then a curious look washed over his face. "Mom, Dad who are they? Are they good guys or bad guys?" Molly and Tom looked at each other. Even though his vision had already deteriorated, they knew Oliver was seeing something they couldn't see. Tom leaned in close to Oliver. "Oh buddy, they're the good guys." He ran his fingers through Oliver's hair. "Definitely the good guys."

Oliver was quiet for a long moment. Then he whispered, "I see Jesus. He wants me to come with Him." Keeping his eyes fixed on what he saw, Oliver said to one of his favorite uncles, "Uncle Matt, come with me." Matt crossed the room and came to Oliver's side. He held Oliver's hand. "It's okay, Oliver, you can go now, and I'll come later." Gently he squeezed his hand. "It's okay."

Oliver was quiet. The clock on the wall ticked, James Taylor music played softly in the background, and the room held muted sounds of prayer. Then, miraculously, Oliver sat up. He hadn't been able to move himself for weeks. His arms reached out in front of him and opened up as if someone were about to hold him. Then in his little voice he said, "Hi, Jesus."

A moment later he lay back down. As Molly held him, his little heart beat for a few more minutes, but she knew he was already gone. And she knew where he was. He had just told them.

. . . .

Oliver's dad, Tom, is my cousin. And Oliver's story is what Jesus often reminds me to remember. It's part of my river experience. Just like John knew he saw a dove and heard a voice, I know a six-year-old can't manufacture his dying experience for the benefit of others. With a cloud of witnesses, Oliver testified to Christ. And when I remember Oliver being lifted into the unseen arms of my unseen Jesus, it makes the realness of another kingdom, another world, another reality more real to me right now.

Oliver's entrance into heaven is what I need to remember when I'm stuck in my three-dimensional world and my vision becomes blurred. It's what I hold on to when doubts shade my heart. It's what I go back to when confusion from this world takes the reins of my thinking.

I know I'm in good company of needing a reminder to remember. At least I know the Twelve around the table needed a good reminder. Jesus gave them tactile props to help them remember too—a broken loaf of bread and a cup of wine. He held them up, looked around the table, and said, "Remember . . ."

He told them to remember because He knew how easy it was going to be for them to forget. He told them to remember because, though He wouldn't be with them in body any longer, He was still real. Real. He's real.

Remember.

Reflections

♦ What is an area in your life where you struggle with doubt? Where do you go and what do you do when you are grappling with spiritual doubts?

_____

_____

_____

_____

_____

_____

_____

_____

_____

♦ One way to help us remember that God is faithful and real is by writing down what God has done in our lives. Journal about things God has done for you. Include answered prayers as well as ways in which He has changed you.

God has done these things for me:

_____

_____

_____

_____

_____

God has answered these prayers:

_____

_____

_____

_____

_____

God has changed me in these ways:

_____

_____

_____

_____

_____

_____

♦ Can any of these remembrances help you face something you currently struggle with?

_____

_____

_____

_____

_____

_____

_____

_____

_____

♦ How do you think God feels about our doubts? Read Matthew 11:2–19. What did Jesus say about John after John asked if Jesus was "the one who was to come, or should we expect someone else?" (v. 3). What do you take away from this reading?

_____

_____

_____

_____

_____

_____

_____

_____

_____

♦ Which part of Oliver's story spoke to you the most? How so?

_____

_____

_____

_____

_____

_____

_____

_____

_____

_____

_____

· ·

God is real. See the proof.

2

Yield

God has plans for you.
Say yes to Him.

"For I know the plans I have for you," declares the LORD,
"plans to prosper you and not to harm you, plans to give
you hope and a future."

JEREMIAH 29:11

I'm a planner. Or at least I used to be. In my younger days, going into a
weekend without a plan was unthinkable. My dad still teases me about
how in high school my best friends and I would come up with the "ultimate plan" for each weekend. It became our tagline; we referred to
it as the U.P. At our senior party we had melon-orange T-shirts made
that said, "The U.P. in Action." Boy, did we think we were cool.

Being a planner was hard on the early years of my marriage. My
husband, Bruce, is more of a wait-and-see-what-I-feel-like-doing-
this-weekend type of guy. This used to drive me insane and was a
source of great disappointment because if my plans didn't go accord-
ingly, I would feel let down and angry.

Having a plan has always made me feel good. It makes me feel purposeful. I feel in control with a plan. I feel like I'm moving toward a specific destination, and that makes me feel productive. So really, if you break it down, my plans are pretty much all about me . . . and making me feel good.

My seventy-five-year-old girlfriend, Bertha, has a saying: "Man proposes, God disposes." Through sharing her own life stories, she's taught me how often our life plans fall apart. Yet, God has an amazing way of graciously putting into place His plans among the rubble of our broken mess. Bertha has shown me what it looks like to lay down self-determined plans and childhood dreams and allow God to reerect His plan.

I have another wise friend, Selma, who's one of the funniest people I've ever met and who's filled with a zillion plans at any given moment. She's a sixty-eight-year-old Southern girl who's going on thirty-five. She rarely hangs out with people her age because they all "act too old." She's an international speaker, teacher, trainer, consultant, Bible study leader, and the list goes on. Wherever she goes she leaves a cloud of dust in the air because she has a way of shaking things up. Yet with all her energy and gusto, she's become skilled at holding her plans loosely, allowing God to interrupt her at His discretion. Here's a Selma story that demonstrates how even our everyday plans need to be pliable, ready to absorb whatever God is up to.

. . . .

"I am sorry, ma'am. That flight has been cancelled," the brunette ticket agent said with a frown, looking down at a computer screen as her fingers flew over the keyboard.

Irritation prickled inside Selma.

"But," the ticket agent brightened, "we can get you on the next flight to El Paso, which leaves at eleven-twenty."

"I guess that's not too bad then," Selma said, glancing at her watch. The vacation Bible school training she was giving wasn't scheduled until 7:00 PM, so she still had plenty of time.

"You'll now be boarding at gate eighteen," the young ticket agent informed her, handing her a ticket.

Selma pulled her red leather purse over her shoulder, picked up her briefcase, and thanked the woman. When she reached the security line, it was a mile long. *I guess this is what I should've expected for a Monday morning*, Selma sighed. After enduring the security hassles, she made her way to the gate, noticing how the airport was teeming with soldiers dressed in uniform.

When she finally boarded the plane, a soldier sitting in her row kindly offered to help her put her briefcase in the overhead compartment. "Thank you so much." She gave him an appreciative smile.

"You're welcome." He had a thick Southern drawl.

"I have a thing about flying; you can lose my clothes but my 'brains' stay with me," she chuckled, settling down into her aisle seat. Feeling cheerful with the airport hassles behind her, she continued, "Are you on leave?"

"Yes, ma'am. Off for two weeks, then back to Iraq." The seat in between them was unoccupied and she felt relieved about this, noticing how large the soldier was. His shoulders spilled into the middle seat and his knees pushed against the seat in front of him.

"Well, I want to thank you for what you are doing for our country."

"It's my pleasure to serve our country."

Selma smiled again at him and then, without warning, huge tears began spilling down his cheeks. Her heart lurched at the sight of this uniformed serviceman crying, and the first thought that popped into her mind was from a conference she'd attended years ago where a legendary football player spoke. Desperate to soothe the soldier, she blurted out her conference wisdom. "It's okay for big boys to cry. Rosie Grier said so!"

"You don't understand." Tears were caught on his long lashes as he dug into his pocket. He pulled out a large solitaire diamond ring and held it toward Selma. "I was going home to surprise her and ask her to marry me." He brushed the tears off his lashes with the back of his hand. "I had this made for her."

"It's gorgeous." Selma leaned over to admire the sparkling white diamond and simple gold band.

"But the day before I left Iraq, I got a 'Dear John' letter." His voice cracked.

A spark of anger ignited in her at the thought of some floozie who couldn't appreciate this soldier putting his life on the line for our country. "I'm so sorry." She pursed her lips and knitted her brow. "That's awful."

Fresh tears sprung in his eyes as he stuffed the ring back inside his pocket. "Ma'am, could you excuse me? I need to use the restroom."

"Of course." Selma scrambled to her feet.

Anxious to do something for this heartbroken young man, she hunted around in her purse and pulled out a Prayer Bear, a little teddy bear she used for vacation Bible school training. It had the name "Jesus" written all over its soft fleece fabric. Selma pulled out a notepad and pen and wrote, "God loves you! I will be praying for you." Each Prayer Bear has a little front pouch, so she folded the note, stuck it inside the bear's pouch, and set it on the soldier's seat.

When the young man came back to his seat, he picked up the bear and looked at her with questioning eyes.

"It's a Prayer Bear for you." She reached over and gave his hand a squeeze. "There's a note for you inside his front pouch too." As he pulled out the note, Selma kept talking. "I want you to remember people are praying for you, and Jesus loves you no matter what."

As the solider read the note, he swallowed hard, and she watched his protruding Adam's apple move up and down the middle of his throat. Hugging the bear to his chest, he whispered, "That's who I've

been leaving out of my life." He swallowed again. "I know better. I'm going to make Him number one in my life again. Thank you."

Emotion swept over her as she watched the soldier hug the soft purple and white bear. Tears filled her eyes and then they were both crying.

"Thank you," he said again with a smile breaking through his tear-stained face.

After they landed in El Paso, the solider hugged Selma and thanked her some more. As he walked away, she grinned when she noticed the head and arms of the Prayer Bear sticking out of his camouflage duffel bag. *Shoot*, she thought, *I didn't even get his name.*

When Selma finally settled into her rental car, it was raining and dreary outside. The church where she was presenting was in a not-so-reputable part of the city, and a large black iron fence surrounded it, making her feel as if she were going to a prison rather than a house of God. She pulled on the gate but it was locked, and she had to wait for a long time until someone finally came to let her in.

As she waited, her sunshiny mood from the morning began to turn the color of the sky. When one of the men in charge of the event eventually led her to where she was to conduct her training workshop, her mood grew a shade dimmer. It was more like a closet than a classroom, barely giving Selma enough room to set up her display. The attendance for her workshop was disappointing, and almost all of those who did attend spoke only Spanish so they had to get an interpreter. Selma felt like most of what she was saying was lost in translation. To complete her letdown, a local pastor told her that her plans to go shopping for jewelry the next day in a little town just south of the Mexican border was risky and ill-advised. He warned her that over the past several months it had become unsafe and recommended she not go.

As she drove to her hotel that night, she felt deflated, like air let out of a balloon. The workshop had been a bust, her shopping adventure had been shot down, and it was still raining. While tossing and turning on her stiff hotel mattress, she decided to quit while she was behind and head to the airport first thing in the morning to try and get on an earlier flight back home.

Selma breathed a prayer the next morning, waiting at the gate as a standby passenger. When they called her name for a seat assignment, she exhaled her gratitude, *Thank You, Lord.* Once on the airplane, she again found herself sitting next to a soldier, who helped her stow her briefcase.

"Where are you going?" he asked cheerfully.

"Fort Worth." Selma wasn't feeling chatty. To give him the hint, she pulled out the airline magazine from the seat pocket in front of her and began flipping through it.

"How long have you been in El Paso?" the soldier tried again.

Without looking up she mumbled, "Just one night."

"Wow. Quick trip. What were you here for?"

Oh please shut up. She clenched her teeth together. "Work."

"Really, what do you do?" His whole body was turned toward her and he seemed oblivious to her borderline rudeness.

"Church resource training."

"Oh, really?" he bubbled. "Oh man! I have to tell you what happened last night. You look like you might need to hear it . . . and you'd understand too." The solider was nearly bobbing up and down in his seat.

Folding up her magazine, Selma surrendered. She could tell he wasn't going to let up so she decided she might as well engage. "Really? What happened?" She made eye contact with him and noticed he was quite handsome with bright blue eyes that reminded her of Paul Newman.

"I went out to dinner with my buddy who's on leave from Iraq. We talked for hours about how we both need to renew our relationship with the Lord."

A wave of guilt swept through her as she realized this young man sitting next to her was eager to talk about the Lord, and she'd almost blown it. "That is so wonderful." Selma nodded with hearty enthusiasm, wanting to make up for her previous disinterest.

"Yeah, we've both sort of drifted over the years, and he's home on leave and just got a 'Dear John' letter."

The soldier now had Selma's full attention. "Really?"

"Yeah." The soldier's face grew serious. "He was pretty devastated, but"—then like a flip of a switch, his face turned bright—"he had the coolest thing happen to him yesterday on a plane."

Selma's heart skipped. "Really?"

"This lady he was sitting next to gave him a Prayer Bear with a prayer note written for him inside of it."

Her mouth fell open, but before she could say anything, the soldier kept talking.

"When we went out last night, we both agreed we needed to make Jesus number one in our lives again, and we decided to recommit ourselves right there in the restaurant!" His clear blue eyes were shining and seemed to turn even bluer as he spoke. "I'm just so mad at my stupid buddy because he didn't get that lady's name or find out where I could get a bear," the soldier sniggered, "cause I want a Prayer Bear too! You know? As a daily reminder for me."

A warm chill permeated through Selma's whole body. Before she could rein in her racing thoughts and respond, the young soldier unbuckled his seat belt. "Ma'am, I drank way too much coffee this morning. I'm sorry to make you get up but I really need to use the restroom."

Still speechless, she got up and let him through. She quickly dug in her purse and snatched a bear. She jotted a quick prayer on a piece of paper, stuffed it in the bear's pouch, and set it on the soldier's seat. *Lord, I cannot believe this!* she whispered under her breath as she stared at the cuddly bear.

A few minutes later the soldier came back, and as he got ready to scoot into his seat, he spotted the bear. "Prayer Bear! Prayer Bear!" His whole face expanded in an explosion of delight. He swirled around looking at the people in the seats and rows around them. "Did you see who put this bear here?" Their area of the plane began to buzz with excitement. When his eyes landed on Selma, he paused for a moment, and then burst, "You're the Prayer Bear lady!"

She nodded her head and he put his enormous hands on her shoulders, squeezing hard.

"Are you real?" His eyes were big and round.

"I won't be if you squeeze any harder," she joked.

He reached over and picked up the bear, brought it to his chest, and hugged it. "Thank you." Tears welled up in both of their eyes. When Selma looked around at others watching them, she saw they weren't the only ones crying.

"I want you to remember that you are being prayed for and God loves you very much," she said as they settled back into their seats.

The soldier nodded, and for the first time all morning he was quiet.

When they got off the plane, the young soldier was telling Selma, and anyone else who'd listen, how he couldn't believe this had happened to him and he couldn't wait to call his buddy and tell him the story. After he hugged Selma good-bye, she watched him walk down the corridor, and a big smile crept up her face when she spied the bear's ears poking out of the soldier's duffel bag. She was sure that bear was smiling.

As Selma drove home, she cried some more. *God, You are something else! I wasn't even supposed to be on either of those planes!* Laughter gurgled up her throat as she thought about her less-than-stellar church training in El Paso and her cancelled shopping spree south of the border. She began giggling until her whole body shook. *Look at what You had planned, Lord! Now there are two soldiers heading back to Iraq with a bear that will remind them of You every single day.*

Truth Dare

. . . .

When I think about Selma's story, I wonder how many opportunities I have missed because I was preoccupied with my own plans, my own agenda. How many times have I walked by someone in the grocery store who was dying on the inside? How many times has someone sitting next to me needed an encouraging word but I was too self-absorbed to discern it? How many times has a neighbor needed me to reach out but I was too busy to notice? I'm sick of missing opportunities! Are you too?

> Many, O LORD my God,
> are the wonders you have done.
> The things you planned for us
> no one can recount to you.
> PSALM 40:5

My husband's cousin Max uses a prayer I love: "God, if You are up to anything fun, please let me be a part of it." It is a fun-loving prayer of an interruptible life. Yet really allowing God's plans to take over our lives is a major shift in operations for many of us. It doesn't mean we sit around with absolutely no direction. It does mean, however, that the plans we do have, the dreams we're pursuing, need to be under His directorship. We need to be seeking His confirmation as we set our course. And once we launch, we need to hold our plans loosely, being available to a change of course if God directs.

Over the past couple of years, I've had the bug to attend seminary and pursue a degree in chaplaincy. My husband and I have had many conversations about this plan, as he had legitimate concerns. It took a long time and many conversations until I felt I had the "go-ahead" I needed to feel okay about my seminary plan. Then I received a partial scholarship, and this seemed like the confirmation I needed to feel better about moving forward.

Finally it was my first day of classes. I was excited to start the new adventure, especially on the same day my husband was getting a contract offer for a great new job. Sometime during my second class, I got a message from Bruce that the job contract fell through, and that his current employer—an Internet start-up company—had just announced they'd run out of funding. Was it coincidence that the day I began seminary Bruce's job situation blew up? I guess this could be debated but I knew with my whole heart that God was telling me "no" to my seminary plan. A few days later I dis-enrolled. Years ago this would have been very difficult for me, to just walk away from something I'd planned out and wanted to do. But now I know that pushing my own agenda and ignoring the Lord's plans never works out in my best interest.

God is up to something in each of our lives. Can we be like Bertha and allow His plans to take root and rebuild the direction of our lives? Can we be like Selma and relinquish our agenda and embrace His opportunities? The real question is, can we dare to believe, really believe, His truth? "'I know the plans I have for you,' declares the Lord, 'plans to prosper you and not to harm you, plans to give you hope and a future'" (Jer. 29:11).

Reflections

"I know the plans I have for you," declares the Lord, "plans to prosper you and not to harm you, plans to give you hope and a future. Then you will call upon me and come and pray to me, and I will listen to you. You will seek me and find me when you seek me with all your heart. I will be found by you," declares the Lord, "and will bring you back from captivity. I

will gather you from all the nations and places where I have banished you," declares the LORD, "and will bring you back to the place from which I carried you into exile." (Jer. 29:11–14)

♦ Earlier in Jeremiah 29, God was telling the Israelites—who had been exiled from their home in Jerusalem and were living in less-than-ideal circumstances—that they must keep on keeping on. God did not want them getting stuck, sitting around waiting for their current situation to get better. He wanted them to live abundantly in their here and now. Do you ever get stuck in going through the motions of your "less than ideal" here and now? Just making it through, waiting until it gets better? How so? Can you apply God's words in Jeremiah 29 to your life? How?

_____

_____

_____

_____

_____

_____

♦ List out some plans you have for the next year of your life.

Goals - joyful grandmothering
self-sufficient garden
healthy eating
Consistant Bible study
See new grandbabies - July & Oct,

_____

♦ Are these plans interruptible? Why or why not?

Yes & No
Can change timing - but should
happen reguardless!

♦ Do you feel like you've <u>missed</u> God-appointed opportunities? Explain.

Sometimes - I can feel myself
to into my "plans" - going toward
my goals instead of looking at what
God is doing & joining in

♦ Which part of Selma's story spoke to you the most? How so?

She thought she was doing God's plan
& He had a whole different purpose

God has plans for you.
Say yes to Him.

3

Revel

**God offers freedom.
Be childlike before Him.**

And he said, "Become like little children."
MATTHEW 18:3

Maybe it's the rules I understood as a child that get the best of me, but when I'm feeling unproductive, I get to feeling vulnerable, and when I'm feeling vulnerable in that way, a voice inside my head switches on, whispering, *You are bad*. And as the wheels start turning, picking up momentum as they spin, pretty soon I'm convinced I'm a bad wife, a bad mother, and an all-around self-centered loser. I've been told by people who know about such things that this inward, downward cycle is commonly referred to as "negative self-talk." Apparently both men and women can be very good at it.

I was with a girlfriend last night who is an admitted professional negative self-talker. She has just come out of her second divorce and can't forgive herself for failing—again. The voice inside her head shrieks, "You are such a messed up, pathetic relational failure. Who

Revel

37

would ever want you? You can't make anything work." She says the only thing that keeps her head above water is having good friends to talk to, people who can take her out of her own head and process truth and reality out loud with her. But when her support people aren't around, the shaming voices grow louder—the water rises higher and she begins to sink.

Why is it so much easier for us to believe a bad-something about ourselves instead of a good-something? Some of the most common bad-somethings we may battle are

I don't matter.

I'm not worth fighting for.

I'm unlovable.

I'm a failure.

If people knew the real me, they wouldn't want me.

If I'm not in control, everything will fall apart.

I'll never be good enough.

How can we be freed from this negative self-talk, or at least not do it as much?

Jesus' teaching—to become like little children—is one way to unhinge ourselves from negative self-talk and bad-somethings. Charlie, my wild and crazy three-year-old nephew, teaches me how to unhinge. When I'm with him, I marvel at his example of being childlike. Jesus told His disciples they must become humble, simple, and childlike.

> Jesus . . . said to them, "Let the little children come to me, and do not hinder them, for the kingdom of God belongs to such as these."
>
> MARK 10:14

Simple, humble Charlie is always in the moment, not pining away on some past failure or hurt. Pining over the past—isn't that what stirs up our negative self-talk? It does for me. Failure and disappointment dangle like Halloween skeletons inside my head. Charlie lives skeleton free. He's all about the here and now, simple and uncomplicated. Jesus beckons us to become like Charlie, not worrying about tomorrow because our Father will take care of us.

Another freedom-from-negative-self-talk factor in Charlie's little life is his uncomplicated dependence. He's the exact opposite of self-sufficient. Because he's the youngest of four, naturally everyone babies him. His mother, father, and three older brothers take care of Charlie's needs—feeding him, bathing him, dressing him, entertaining him. And his sweet dependency is an integral piece of his freedom. Jesus chides us, *become like Charlie, lean on Me, dependent, needy . . . I can give you rest.*

To top it all off, Charlie is the spongelike recipient of adoration. Being the baby, he is the love object of his whole family. His daily experience is that of being cherished. Without knowing it, Charlie illustrates what Jesus means to become like a child and revel in our Father's love—and *live* from that place.

Jennifer, a gal I was introduced to by a good friend, is a believer just like Charlie. She believes she's a cherished child of God, and from this place she has dared to live . . . skeleton free, dependent on God, without a distorted self-perception. She doesn't get bogged down by belaboring her regrets or by hosting a pity party for herself. She isn't into negative self-talk or self-condemnation. She's a child of God. Period. She's loved and adored. Period. Just like I marvel at Charlie, I marvel and learn from Jennifer's childlike freedom.

. . . .

"I'll be back before you know it!" Gloria blew on the hot cider in her mug, and then took a sip.

"Mom, it's okay," sixteen-year-old Jennifer swiped her brown bangs away from her forehead. "Really."

"I still wish you weren't going to be gone over Christmas," Jonelle's twelve-year-old face fell into a pout.

"I know, honey. Neither do I. But Oma and Opa have been sick, and I haven't seen them in a long time."

"It will go by quickly." Jim gave an encouraging nod toward his youngest daughter. "Plus, we've got a lot to do while she's gone. You've got your choir concert tonight and finals this week, and we have shopping to get done."

"Besides," Gloria said, "we'll have only one extra day to wait until we celebrate together. I'll be back on the twenty-sixth!" She glanced at her watch. "The shuttle should be here any minute." She stood up. "Let me hug you girls now." She wrapped her arms around Jonelle. "Bye, sweetie. I love you." Then she hugged Jennifer. "Good luck in your game tonight. Love you, sweetie."

Jim helped Gloria get her suitcase out the front door. "I'll call when I get there," she promised, giving her husband a kiss.

As Gloria's airport shuttle pulled out of the driveway, Jennifer bolted upstairs to change into her basketball uniform. A minute later Jonelle barged into her room. "Can I please borrow this tonight?" She held up a long gray down coat. "I have nothing else to wear and it goes perfectly with my outfit."

"No. Wear your own coat." Jennifer brushed her hair back into a ponytail.

"Just for tonight?" Jonelle's voice raised an octave higher.

"No!" Jennifer snatched the coat from Jonelle and headed downstairs. "I'm leaving, Dad," she called over her shoulder, ignoring Jonelle's whining pleas behind her.

"Good luck, honey! After I drop off Jonelle at school, I'll be at your game."

"I let you borrow my stuff!" Jonelle shrieked.

Truth Dare

Jennifer rolled her eyes. "You do not." She left through the garage door and even after it closed behind her, she could hear Jonelle ranting.

A half hour later, Jim took Jonelle through the McDonald's drive-thru for a quick pre-concert dinner. "I'll be home about an hour after the Rosses drop you off," he told her as she munched on salty fries. As soon as Jim watched his daughter board the school bus, he headed for Greeley Central High School where Jennifer's varsity game had already begun.

After losing a close game, Jennifer went to Taco Bell with some friends while Jim drove home. "Hi, Jonelle," Jim called as he walked into the house and set his keys on the kitchen countertop. When she didn't answer, Jim tried again. "Jone-E-el." Still there was no answer. He could hear the television on downstairs in their family room. He went to the top of the stairs. "Hi, Jonelle."

No answer.

His mouth formed a straight line. "Jonelle?" He walked down the stairs. In front of the television he saw her nylon stockings in a pile on the floor, and he noticed the quartz heater next to their leather chair was turned on, but Jonelle was not there.

Frowning, Jim walked back upstairs. For several minutes he searched the house, calling out her name. His brow furrowed as he went outside. "Jonelle?" he called from the back of the house. It was a cold night and several inches of snow covered the ground. Their house backed up to open fields, and Jim's voice cut through the darkness.

After repeatedly calling for her, he went back inside and telephoned his good friend and pastor, Jim Christy. In a steady voice he explained the situation.

"Have you called the family who dropped Jonelle off after the choir concert?" Pastor Jim asked.

"No, I haven't." His eyes locked on the side door to the garage, hoping Jonelle would walk in.

"I'd try that. And if they don't know anything, I wouldn't hesitate to call the police, Jim."

Jim hung up and called the Ross family. He learned that they'd dropped Jonelle off around 8:20 PM and hadn't talked to her since. A short time later, when Jennifer arrived home, Jim had already called the police.

"Honey, do you have any idea where Jonelle might be?" Jim asked as Jennifer slipped off her coat and tossed it over a kitchen chair.

"No. Why?"

While Jim was explaining to Jennifer, the doorbell rang. He opened the door and two policemen stepped inside the front hallway, their black boots covered with snow. "When was the last time anyone saw Jonelle?" the taller police officer asked as he flipped open a notepad. After listening for a while, Jennifer slipped upstairs to her bedroom and called her boyfriend, Nathan.

"Jonelle is missing," Jennifer said, sitting down on top of her bed, cross-legged.

"What?"

"Dad came home and her stuff was here but she was gone. The police are here." Jennifer kept her voice low as she relayed the story to Nathan. While they were talking, she heard a knock on her bedroom door. She turned to see one of the policemen standing in her doorway.

"Excuse me. I was wondering if I could ask you a few questions?"

"Uh, sure." She stood up. "Nathan, I need to call you back." She hung up and turned toward the policeman.

"What did you do tonight while Jonelle was at her choir concert?" The officer held his pen, ready to take notes.

"I played a basketball game." Her eyes glanced at the black gun holstered on his hip.

"Where?"

"At the high school."

"Do you have any idea where your sister might be?"

Jennifer shook her head. "No."

After ten more minutes of questions, the officer thanked Jennifer. "I'm going to look through Jonelle's room."

"Sure," Jennifer said, pointing to her sister's room, "it's just next to mine."

For hours the police officers combed the house, lifting fingerprints from the family room, the kitchen, and bedrooms. Then they searched outside with big black flashlights. As the night wore on, pieces of evidence indicated that someone had broken into their home. First they found someone had gone through Gloria's jewelry box. Next they discovered a set of footprints leading up to the lower-level windows. The prints didn't appear to match anyone in the family.

Jennifer waited up with her dad as the police continued to search for clues. They were both stoic and quiet as they waited. Finally, after midnight, Jennifer told her dad she was going to bed. With the police still collecting information, Jennifer shut the door to her room and pulled off her basketball uniform, slipping on a nightshirt and sweat-pants. As she tugged her comforter over her, she could hear the police radios transmitting loud dispatch information.

This is so weird, she thought, staring up at the ceiling. She felt detached from what was going on, like she was in the middle of someone else's bizarre dream. When the phone rang, Jennifer strained to hear through the vent on her bedroom floor what her dad was saying. She could tell by the way he talked that it was her mom on the other end of the line. She rolled onto her side and closed her eyes as a ripple of sadness washed over her. *Poor Mom. She's going to be so worried.*

The next morning when Jennifer woke up, Jonelle was still missing and more police were in their home. Although her dad was a calm man, Jennifer could feel his worry like a thick smoke filling the house. "What did Mom say?" Jennifer's eyes followed her dad as he walked to the cupboard and pulled out a tin can of coffee.

"She's coming home. She should be here by this afternoon."

"Should I go to school?"

"I think so. It doesn't make a lot of sense for you to stay home." The color was drained from his face.

A half an hour later, a police officer drove Jennifer to school. Teachers already seemed to know Jonelle was missing and gave Jennifer extra attention and care. By the time Jennifer got home that afternoon, her mom was there and so were a handful of detectives and numerous reporters. Over the next few days, Jennifer felt their lives swept into a surreal whirlwind. The media was camped out at their house at all hours of the day and night. Jim and Gloria were both in front of various television cameras, asking that if anyone had seen their daughter, to please contact the police. A "Rescue Jonelle" task force was set up. Various search crews with hundreds of volunteers were organized. Flyers with Jonelle's picture were printed and distributed. Rewards were promised. Donations were given. *Unsolved Mysteries* even flew a crew out to film a story about Jonelle for their show.

But weeks passed without a trace of Jonelle.

One night more than a month after Jonelle disappeared, the house seemed particularly empty and sad. Jennifer sat on her bed, holding a new journal. She opened it and on the dedication page wrote,

> Jenni Mathews
> for
> Jonelle
> Feb. 4, 1985

She turned to the next page and continued.

> Jonelle:
> I have had a lot of feelings run through my head since you've been gone. Mixed feelings about hundreds of things go through my mind—especially about different people and

naturally—you! I think you ought to know just how I feel—
so this journal is for you.
Jenni

Her emotions felt like they were churning in a blender on high
speed. Chunks of guilt tumbled with lumps of sorrow blended with
bits of resentment and anger. *I just wish this would end.* She turned
off her lamp and slid underneath her comforter. Through the vent
she heard the muffled sobs of her mother. Her parents' room was underneath hers, and she knew her mom always waited to cry when she
thought Jennifer couldn't hear her. The problem was she could hear.
Hugging her knees to her chest, Jennifer cried too.

A couple of nights later, Jennifer was home alone. Gloria and
Jim had gone to meet with a missing-children advocate group, and
Jennifer once again felt the absence of Jonelle echoing loudly off the
too-quiet walls of their home. She flopped down on her bed, opened
her journal, and began to write.

Feb. 6
During this month and a half, I've thought a lot about how
we used to act toward each other. All the fights we had over
stupid little things, like borrowing clothes, using the phone,
etc. It's only natural for sisters to do that, but if we really
stop and think about it—we really do love each other. It
takes times like these to make it more evident.

You really don't realize what you have until it's gone, and
since you're gone, I kinda miss those arguments. At least
there wasn't this void like there is now. I don't have to wake
anyone up at 6:30 or get out of the bathroom for anyone so
they can use it. It's really kind of boring. In your own way
you kept me on my toes. I just hope it is not too late to tell
you how much I love you.

As Jennifer wrote, a heaviness filled her chest. She put down her pen and stared at the wall of her bedroom. *I just wish she was here, asking me to borrow something so I could say yes!*

The next day after school Jennifer found herself driving to church. She realized she wanted and *needed* to talk to Pastor Jim. She parked her car in the near-empty lot and walked into the front office. The moment Pastor Jim saw Jennifer, a welcoming smile spread across his face. "Jennifer!"

"I was wondering if you had a few minutes?"

"Of course!" He ushered her into his zebra-themed office. She sank down on a black leather chair in front of his desk and took a deep breath. "I just feel so guilty." Jennifer looked across the desk at Pastor Jim. His eyes were kind and gentle. His snow-white hair accentuated his wise, reassuring demeanor. "I could have been so much nicer to her."

"Jenni, you know she was a difficult person. Jonelle was hard to get along with at times."

"But why couldn't I have been nicer? The very last time I was with her, we had a fight . . ." Jennifer's voice trailed away.

"You can't be so hard on yourself. You need to remember that sisters know how to push each other's buttons. Don't beat yourself up."

Jennifer could see the sincerity of his words etched into the lines of his face. As he spoke, it was like her thirsty heart was drinking a cup of cold water.

"You need to forgive yourself," he continued. "Sisters fight. Jonelle was difficult. You can't burden yourself with guilt. Jennifer . . . ," Pastor Jim paused for a moment. "Jonelle knew you loved her. She loved you too."

Jennifer swallowed the lump that had risen in her throat and nodded.

"Let's pray." Pastor Jim bowed his head. "Lord, I pray Jennifer does not allow guilt and condemnation to haunt her. There is no

condemnation in You . . ." as he continued, a comforting peace dripped over Jennifer like a fragrant spring rain.

When she left Pastor Jim's office a few minutes later, she inhaled the cold air deep into her lungs. Though the temperature was frigid outside, her insides felt warmer, her conscience lighter. *He's right*, she thought, starting the engine. *It's no good to feel so guilty . . . I can't live this way.* While waiting for the car to warm up, she stared out the car window to the west, soaking in the snow-covered mountains and crystal blue sky. Moving the gearshift into reverse, she whispered, "I love you, Jonelle. Wherever you are."

Weeks turned into months turned into years and Jonelle never came home. She was never found. Jennifer continued to feel a piercing sense of loss and sadness, yet she learned how to believe the truths of Pastor Jim's words, permitting them to quietly shape who she became and how she lived. She didn't allow guilt or regret to take root. She turned her back on negative self-talk and learned not to beat herself up for what she could not change. She humbled herself like a child, dependent and trusting her Father. And a place called Freedom is where she lives.

. . . .

When Jesus told the disciples to become like children, He was answering their self-absorbed question, "Who will rank the greatest in the kingdom of God?" Jesus replied, "Those who become like children will be the greatest" (see Matt. 18:1–4).

Fascinating that those who will be the greatest in God's kingdom will be like children—forgiving, humble, elemental, dependent, needy, absent of pride, and free from self-condemnation.

I've tried to put myself in Jennifer's situation, and I'm afraid that, thirty years after my sister's disappearance, I'd look nothing like her. I'm afraid if I were her, I'd walk surrounded by a haze of guilt, kind of like Pigpen in Charlie Brown whose hazy cloud of dirt always follows him. I'm afraid I'd never forgive myself for not letting her borrow my coat the last time we were together. I'm afraid that underneath the surface of my Christian veneer would fester a deep vat where self-loathing grew like a nasty bacterial infection. In other words, I'm afraid I'd live my life a captive in a place where I allowed the sin of self-loathing and condemnation to administer the state of my internal affairs.

But I want to be like Jennifer. I want to live in freedom and say no to the "you are bad" voice inside my head. And that's where becoming like a child drops into the picture. A little child does not beat herself up for the past. Charlie, when he's naughty, gets corrected and moves on. You don't hear him saying, "I'm such a bad boy. I always mess up. Mommy could never love me." He's humble. He gets that his mom's and dad's love is bigger than what he does or doesn't do.

Jennifer's freedom, too, comes from knowing that God is bigger than any of her "should-haves" or "shouldn't-haves." He's bigger than her yesterday. Negative self-talk and self-condemnation fester when we don't hand over our yesterdays to God. God cannot redeem what we do not give Him.

My friend Nancy shared with me a meditation that focuses on how God is eager to forgive us. After reading this meditation, I pondered on how little children wouldn't need to do this exercise. They get it. Yet somewhere along the way as we grow up, we lose it. And we need to relearn it—God is all about wiping away yesterday's should-haves and shouldn't-haves. When we don't allow Him to do this, we shut off places in our hearts and lose the capacity to live in the freedom He offers.

Become like little children.

It's a place where there is no room for self-condemnation.

It's a place of truth and freedom. It's a place where Jennifer and Charlie live.

Reflections

♦ Below are some descriptions about children. Circle the ones that describe you. Consider the ones that are not circled. Why are these qualities are difficult for you?

Trusting	(Genuine)
Teachable	(Expressive)
Dependent	Believing
Imaginative	(Silly)
(Honest)	Carefree
Playful	Unhurried
Unstressed	

trusty — been betrayed

teachable — headstrong ~

Dependant — people let me down

imaginative — waste of time

playful — too busy

unstressed — like stress

believing — sceptical

confused — busy

unhurried — no time

♦ In what area of life do you struggle with negative self-talk? Describe your struggle.

parenting Daykota — feel hopeless sometimes

♦ Romans 8:1, "There is no <u>condemnation</u> for those who are in Christ," is a well-known verse. Do you think "those who are in Christ" live this way? Treat one another this way? <u>What does this verse mean?</u> How does it look to live this way?

We shouldn't be condemning others

♦ Which part of Jennifer's story spoke to you the most? How so?

**God offers freedom.
Be childlike before Him.**

4

Pause

**God knows what's best for you.
Wait for His direction.**

Wait for the LORD;
Be strong and let your heart take courage;
Yes, wait for the LORD.

PSALM 27:14 (NASB)

The other night I picked up an Oswald Chambers book, *My Utmost for His Highest*. Inscribed in the front of the book is an encouraging note from my first youth leader, whom I met in tenth grade right after I became a Christian. I've read bits and pieces from this devotional during the thirty-some years I've been journeying with Christ. In my most recent skimming, something struck me anew that I'd read before but never really noticed:

> There are times when you cannot understand why you cannot do what you want to do. When God brings that blank space,

see that you *do not fill it in*, but wait. . . . Never run before God's guidance. (Emphasis added)

An unknown . . . a future uncertainty . . . not getting what we want when we want it. How often do you fill in the blank space in your own life? Personally, I'm a huge fill-in-the-blank gal. Learning to be okay with a blank space has been a brutal and slow process. But the longer I've lived with Christ, the more I've learned that when I fill in the blank, instead of allowing God to fill it in, things usually don't go so well. Know what I mean?

Here's the thing with not filling in the blank—you have to be patient. You have to learn to wait on the Lord and allow Him to fill in the blank for you. Who is naturally good at waiting? Is anyone good at this? Last night I dropped off my son at a friend's house for a Super Bowl party, and I had a hard time waiting when a pizza delivery guy pulled up behind me, blocking my car while he ran inside to deliver the boys' pizza. I sat there less than five minutes, yet waiting felt like a slice of eternity. I sighed, I moaned, I fidgeted, I grumbled under my breath, I got out of the car and paced. No, waiting has never been my strength. I'm the woman pushing the cart through the grocery store, ripping into a bag of something because I can't wait to eat until I get home.

But waiting on the Lord to give His answer, His guidance, His direction is a discipline I've slowly been cultivating over many years. And when I wait—when I don't rush ahead and fill in the blank, when I don't force my answer—peace saturates me instead of the old familiar angst.

I met a gal several years ago who has an amazing story about waiting, about not filling in the blank with her answer—or anybody else's answer for that matter—but allowing God to fill it in for her. Her name is Ruth.

. . . .

It was late, but Ruth was in the habit of staying up to wait for her husband, Jonathon, to hear how that evening's performance had gone. For the past year, Jonathon had gotten to play many leading roles at a distinguished theater in Paris, France. He had a swing role, which meant he was a backup for any member of the ensemble cast. A stay-at-home mom with their baby boy, Ruth craved adult interaction. She didn't speak the language and felt increasingly isolated and lonely during their year and a half abroad. She looked forward to hearing about the excitement in Jonathon's world when he got home every night. When the phone rang at 10:30, Ruth's heart sank. *He's going out again with the cast,* she thought as she picked up the phone.

"Hello."

"Hi."

"You okay?" Something in his voice made her heart flutter.

"I need to talk to you."

An alarm sounded inside Ruth's head. "Okay."

"I'm coming home now."

When Ruth set the phone down, she drew a shaky breath. All of Jonathon's odd behavior over the past few months rushed to the front of her mind like a violent gust of wind. He'd become progressively moody and withdrawn. A cold knot formed in her stomach as she thought about how much time he'd begun taking to get ready for work. At first she had dismissed it, but lately it had become so obvious that it was impossible to ignore. He had also developed a skin rash in the past month and told her it was stress related. Adding to all of that, his ability to be intimate with her had increasingly waned.

Just last week they had tried to be intimate, but after a few minutes, Jonathon had pulled away.

"Are you having an affair?" Ruth had asked.

"No."

"Because if you're not wanting to have sex at home, that makes me think you're getting it somewhere else."

"No."

"Are you sure?"

"Yes. I'm just depressed. Not myself." His dejected voice had softened her heart and she had reached over and stroked his hair.

As she ran her fingers through his hair, she had given herself a silent lecture. He's just going through a really stressful time. I need to be more understanding. He's always been honest with me, and I need to trust that.

When Jonathon opened the front door to their apartment, it startled Ruth out of her dark thoughts. But, looking into his face, she knew. "You're having an affair."

"Yes. I am."

"With Karen?"

"No."

"With Alan?"

"Yes."

"I feel like I'm going to throw up." She staggered into the bathroom and bent over the toilet. Gagging, she tried to make the vomit come up that she tasted at the back of her throat. But it wouldn't. Finally she rinsed her mouth, went into their small family room, and collapsed on the couch. Tears poured down her cheeks. "How long?"

"Since October."

She cupped her face in her hands as choking sobs erupted from her broken heart. *Nooo!* her mind screamed. *For six months he's been having a homosexual affair!* Again the bile rose up in her throat.

As she wept, she thought about the handful of times Jonathon had come to her and confessed his internal pull toward homosexuality. He had always felt horrible and shameful about his silent struggle. Ruth had wanted the perfect marriage, and since this problem with Jonathon was something that didn't fit that image, each time he brought it up she'd been quick to forgive him and dismiss the whole thing.

Wrapping her arms around herself, she rocked back and forth. Her thoughts shifted to Alan, and she gagged again. Over the past month she'd read some e-mails that Alan had sent to Jonathon. They had disturbed her. They seemed too personal. Too intimate. But once again she'd discounted her feelings and tried harder to be a good wife.

Panic rose inside her like a tidal wave. Looking up at Jonathon, she tried to talk but the words jammed in her throat. Finally she whispered, "What have you decided?"

"I don't know. Alan supported me telling you and said he'll be there for me."

His words made a direct hit on her heart, nearly knocking the wind out of her. Sobs took control of her again. Finally, after her weeping settled down, she spoke. "I don't want this to be the end of our marriage." She looked into her husband's eyes. He looked away.

For a moment, compassion swelled inside her. She saw the anguish etched in his profile. And she knew him. She knew his heart. He was a good man. He loved God. He was kind. She knew Satan was waging war with Jonathon. Even though Jonathon was buying into Satan's lies, she didn't.

"We have Seth. We're a family."

Jonathon didn't respond.

"What about our trip?"

"I want you and Seth to go but I won't be coming. I think it would be good to have a separation. I need time to think."

Ruth's heart plunged. For months they'd planned to go back to the States to be with family. She didn't want to go alone. She wanted to go with Jonathon.

What should I do, Lord? If I go alone, that will give Jonathon and Alan the green light to do whatever they want. That'll probably just cinch their relationship. Sorrow and fear smothered her.

Ruth's next two weeks were full of pain. Although she didn't want to go back to the States without Jonathon, she felt God fill in the blank for her with a steady whisper, telling her, *Go*. Once she was back in the States, she was faced with another blank space about what to do next. There were all sorts of options: stay in the States and grant Jonathon the separation he wanted; divorce Jonathon—after all, there were solid biblical grounds for that; take Seth and go back to France, hoping and praying Jonathon would turn around.

Ruth received a myriad of counsel about what to do from wonderful church people, but she strained to listen to the steadfast voice inside her, the voice of the Holy Spirit. And once again she heard His whisper. *Go back*.

When Ruth went back to France, she found Jonathon still deeply entwined in his relationship with Alan. She asked him to move out until he chose to end the affair. Jonathon moved in with Alan, who happened to live in the same apartment complex. Ruth had no idea how long she could stand the daily in-her-face anguish, especially without any family or friends nearby, but she knew it was where God wanted her to be—for now.

So she waited. Most mornings it was like waking up to a nightmare. She couldn't sleep well and had no appetite as the uncertainty of her future weighed down on her.

> Therefore we do not lose heart. Though outwardly we are wasting away, yet inwardly we are being renewed day by day. For our light and momentary troubles are achieving for us an eternal glory that far outweighs them all.
>
> 2 CORINTHIANS 4:16–17
>
> (THESE ARE THE VERSES RUTH MEMORIZED AND RECITED WHILE WAITING FOR JONATHON TO MAKE UP HIS MIND.)

One afternoon she sat out on her apartment balcony while Seth napped. Her Bible had become her lifeline and lay open in her lap. In her mind she allowed herself to play out the worst-case scenario of her situation: her marriage ending and raising Seth alone. As her mind wrapped around the idea of life as a single mom, an unexpected peace, warm and certain, eased over her. *We're going to be okay.* She let out a long, slow breath. *You're going to take care of us no matter what, aren't You?* She looked up past the treetops into the sky and dabbed at two tears. A gentle wind rustled the leaves. Ruth closed her eyes. *So how long do I stay here, Lord, and live like this?*

Again she waited for Him to fill in the blank.

Ruth stayed for three months. Although every day was full of pain, in some strange way she felt more in control of her dreadful circumstances. But during another afternoon on the balcony, she felt God whisper into her heart that it was time to leave. *You've accomplished what I needed you to do. It's time for Jonathon to be alone.*

"But Lord, if I'm here, he has to face the repercussions of his decisions. He has to see Seth every day, and it helps him realize what he'd be losing."

It's time. Go back home.

Ruth swallowed the lump in her throat as tears filled her eyes. In the back of her mind, she knew she couldn't change Jonathon's heart or save her marriage. It was between Jonathon and God. But leaving France felt so passive and so permanent.

Ruth allowed God's direction to sink in and guide her. She informed Jonathon of her decision and moved back to the United States with Seth.

In a long, excruciating process over the next several months, Jonathon turned away from Alan and back to his marriage. Full reconciliation was a complicated progression for Jonathon and Ruth, but with both their hearts opened and humbled before God, and with good counseling, they gradually were able to bring their family back together.

Today, many years later, Ruth reflects on waiting on God during that grueling season of her life: "I knew one thing—I was not going to leave my marriage until God told me to. No matter what other people told me to do or not to do, until He released me from my marriage, I was not released. I needed to wait on Him throughout the whole thing and allow Him to provide the direction and instructions about what to do next. In many ways it was a good thing that I was all alone in a foreign country because God was all I had. I turned to Him with everything."

. . . .

Learning to *not* fill in the blank is tricky business. If I had been in Ruth's situation, I'm sure I would have gotten divorced. I'm sure I would have looked at the Bible and said to myself, *Well, here it is. It says if your spouse commits adultery, you can divorce him. Not to mention homosexual adultery. So there. Divorce.*

I probably would have surrounded myself with Christians who would have said what I wanted them to say, and I would have used that as my confirmation. This attitude doesn't leave any room for God's Spirit to speak to me.

Often what we think is right is dead wrong.

Peter wanted to stop Jesus from going to the cross because that seemed right to him. Martha wanted Mary to help her in the kitchen because that seemed right to her. Both were wrong.

Divorcing Jonathon may have seemed right to many bystanders looking in on Ruth's life. But instead of filling in the blank with what others thought or with what seemed right, she waited. She listened. She was open to hear God's Spirit when He spoke to her. She learned how God's guidance is fluid. It wasn't a onetime answer, a final here's-what-to-do. She received different answers at different times, which meant Ruth had to learn how to dance with the Holy Spirit.

Years ago I talked my husband into taking dance lessons with me. Dancing is not his thing, but he went because I really wanted to take the lessons. It wasn't long before we had to quit the ten-week session because we'd end up in a fight after each lesson. It turns out I was a horrible dance partner. Even though the dance instructor repeatedly told me to allow Bruce to lead the dance, I would inevitably forget and try to take over. Even when I was concentrating on following Bruce's lead, I would subtly slip into lead mode. We quickly discovered how exasperating it is to have two leaders when you're dancing.

It's the same with the Holy Spirit. Dancing with Him requires allowing Him to lead. Yielding to His lead often means we don't know exactly where we are going or when we might get there. Most of us don't like this. We like to be in control and call the shots. We hate unknowns. We have to learn to follow the Spirit's lead anyway.

Another critical piece of Ruth's wait-on-God story is the listening component, which goes hand in hand with the not-calling-the-shots component. The word *listen* is a verb. Listening is an action. It requires being engaged. We need to listen to God in the same way I needed to listen to Bruce on the dance floor by following his movements and unspoken direction. Fully at attention. Waiting for His response.

Maybe you're like me, and one of the reasons it's hard to listen to God is the distraction of multiple voices talking at the same time. It's difficult for me to listen *well* to more than one person talking at the same time. I often have to stop all three of my children from talking at once and call on them one at a time. And after twenty-four years of marriage, Bruce still doesn't fully understand that my brain simply cannot process him talking to me while I'm also talking on the phone. Whenever he does this (which isn't often anymore), I end up hearing fragments of sentences and get irritated. I cannot listen effectively to two people talking to me at the same time. Likewise, Ruth could not listen well to God and the voices of others at the same time. She had to turn up the volume with God by being alone with Him. Just Him.

Have you ever noticed how Jesus spent the whole night in prayer the day before He chose His twelve apostles? You can read the story in Luke 6. A whole night devoted to prayer, listening to one voice, before making a big decision. That inspires me. I want to do that more. I want to break away and get in front of God for hours at a time when I have blank space looming in front of me. Just like Jesus. Just like Ruth. One voice. Breaking away and listening to Him.

After a lot of exhausting and painful work, Ruth and Jonathon's marriage is now whole and healed, and they have three beautiful boys. Waiting on God opened the doors to their reconciliation. Like Ruth, we need to cleave to the psalmist's words:

> Wait for the LORD; Be strong and let your heart take courage;
> Yes, wait for the LORD.
>
> Psalm 27:14 (NASB)

Reflections

♦ In spite of our modern, instant-messaging, ultra-impatient society, life is full of waiting. Yet one of the most challenging instructions and patterns of life we find in Scripture is to "wait" on God. Although most of us hate to wait, waiting has many benefits. Think about periods in your life when you've had to wait. In hindsight, can you see advantages from your times of waiting? Describe these.

Waiting in lines — offices — learnt to pray for those around us

_____

_____

_____

_____

♦ Reread the Oswald Chambers quote on pages 50–51. How do his words connect with your own life?

_____

_____

_____

_____

_____

_____

♦ Are you in a "waiting" period right now? Explain.

_____

_____

_____

_____

_____

_____

♦ What is hardest for you when it comes to waiting on the Lord?

Trying not to figure it out

_____

_____

_____

_____

♦ In *The Amplified Bible*, Isaiah 40:31 says, "But those who wait for the LORD [who expect, look for, and hope in Him] shall change and renew their strength and power; they shall lift their wings and mount up [close to God] as eagles [mount up to the sun]; they shall run and not be weary, they shall walk and not faint or become tired." Describe how you could apply this verse to an area of your life.

_____

_____

_____

_____

_____

_____

_____

_____

♦ Which part of Ruth's story spoke to you the most? How so?

Her willingness to be used of God in walk the rough road — when she had scripture grounds to walk away (an easier out)

_____

_____

_____

· ·

**God knows what's best for you.
Wait for His direction.**

5

Die

**God wants to give you *life!*
Lose yourself to Him.**

Whoever finds his life will lose it, and whoever
loses his life for my sake will find it.
MATTHEW 10:39

When my aunt Nancy was in the final stages of breast cancer, she told my cousin Becky, who is her oldest daughter, that she wanted to "do this well." It's been many years since she died, yet I've often thought about how she wanted to die well. It fits her, really. She lived well, so of course she would want to die well.

It makes me wonder about dying well in my own life. And not just when I'm actually, physically dying like my aunt Nancy, but dying while I am living too. Jesus tells us we need to die in order to live, to lose our life—forget about ourselves, stop clinging to life—to find life. While the world screams, "*Come live!*" Jesus beckons gently, "Come die."

Polar opposite messages really, and most days I feel like a struggling wannabe—vacillating somewhere between living like the world urges and dying like Jesus invites.

I have a deep fascination with Mother Teresa, and at times I've fantasized what it would be like to be young and single, sell everything, move to India to join a Mother Teresa operation, and work with the dying. In my fantasy it seems wonderful—simply serving, not worrying about anything of the world, like putting on my mascara before I go out in public so someone doesn't ask me if I'm tired.

But could I really live that way? Just serving humbly, looking tired, and dying to myself? I always believed I had enough passion for Jesus in me that I could have been one of Mother Teresa's best girls. Then came Peru.

A year ago I went to Peru on a mission trip. It was an all women's trip, with the exception of police escorts and translators. We traveled down a remote tributary of the Amazon River to a village of about seventy families. Before the trip, I was nervously excited to go on a ten-day adventure—to leave behind my kids and husband and just be with Jesus, serving others less fortunate. I was teed up for a week of humble service, dying to myself, all Mother Teresa–like.

I'm still stunned by what happened on the trip. I froze. I failed. I fell apart. I wanted to go home. I hated being fifteen hours up some remote tributary of muddy brown water with women I didn't know, villagers I couldn't communicate with, and work that seemed very American and inconsequential—beading/art projects, some hygiene tutelage, and language-challenged Bible study with the women. My vision of "just being with Jesus" as I served was a bust because the scream in my own head to "get me out of here" was so loud I couldn't focus on anything else. I felt like the baby bird in the P. D. Eastman book *Are You My Mother?* when it screams, "I want to go home! I want my mother!"

I need to underscore that the mission trip was actually a wonderful experience for the women in our group and the village women. My

learning Spanish
CD - Montana
Blackship - Experiencing God
83
17
Summer of 2000

Anyone have a story like this?

personal experience was a reflection of what God was digging up in me, and not an indication of a poorly planned trip.

So what happened to me? Why couldn't I just serve humbly for a week? My bust of a mission trip can be explained by a lot of "oh, that makes sense" reasons. First, staying on a boat in close quarters led me to discover that I'm claustrophobic. Second, I somehow forgot my inhaled steroid asthma medicine, and as a lifelong asthmatic I knew this could be a major problem. My son was airlifted by a Flight for Life helicopter this summer for an asthma attack. I knew if my asthma got to a critical point, I would have no Flight for Life option.

Third, the work we were doing made me want to fling myself out of the boat. I've decided I'm definitely wired for more of a hammer-and-nails, build-something-to-leave-behind type of mission trip. When I signed up for the trip, I understood it to be a conglomeration of different types of service. In our original prepare-for-the-trip manual, we were told to bring work gloves and tools, indicating we'd be doing some physical labor. We did none, and as a result I became restless and anxious—so much so that I begged the trip leader to ask the Peruvian boat crew to please lend me a broom so I could sweep the decks for them. (I found out later the very good reason we didn't do any physical labor: it would have made the villagers feel uneasy to have a group of women doing their "men's work.")

To top it all off, the inability to communicate with the villagers, who spoke a Spanish dialect, left me, a story-writer, incredibly frustrated. I had hundreds of questions I wanted to ask them but couldn't.

Despite all the seemingly good explanations for my lousy mission experience, I felt God nudge me repeatedly that there was more to my implosion. I spent weeks processing it and even met with a counselor to try and unpack what went so very wrong for me. Why did I fail so miserably? Why couldn't I just get over myself and serve for a lousy week?

One thing I've uncovered is that I was in cling overdrive. The New Living Translation of Matthew 10:39 reads, "If you cling to your life, you will lose it; but if you give up your life for me, you will find it." I was clinging to my expectations of what I thought the trip would be. I was clinging to my own securities of being useful and connected. I was clinging to home and my husband and kids. And as I clung, my connection with God went dead, like a dropped cell phone call. There was no signal. I was lost and afraid.

So how do we wake up every morning and not cling to our lives? How do we wake up and die with Him? What does that look like? If you're not Mother Teresa, or don't even have the capability of being one of her best girls, can you still come-die-with-Jesus in the chaos of our self-absorbed society?

For the past year I've been meeting with Vickie, a forty-something mom of four who is dying of Lou Gehrig's disease. Each time I meet with her, she tells me about her life while I type wildly on my laptop. Then later, when I'm at home, I take what I've typed and write pieces of her unofficial memoir—moments from her life, memories, things she wants her children to know and hold on to after she's gone. I make postings for her blog site and chronicle her spiritual journey so her kids will have important pieces of their mom's story.

Vickie has taught me a big part of what it means to die well. Not just because she *is* dying but more because of how she is living. She has found a way to take Jesus' words—to lose her life, to stop clinging—and make them her reality.

. . . .

"Time to do your hair." Vickie reached over the bathtub to get the shampoo for her daughter.

"I want the strawberry kind," seven-year-old Morgan requested as she poured soap from a plastic Mickey Mouse bottle onto her tummy and began to rub with vigor.

"Here, sweetie. Let's—" but before Vickie could finish what she was saying, her legs buckled and she crumpled to the bathroom floor, bringing the shower curtain down with her.

"Mommy!" screeched Morgan.

"It's okay, honey." Vickie pretended everything was normal. "I'll call Daddy to help us. *Tommy!*" Vickie bellowed for her husband. "It's okay," she reassured Morgan, who stood in the tub, dripping with water.

"What happened?" Tommy hurried to Vickie's side, kneeling down on the tile floor.

"I was just reaching to get the shampoo for Morgan, and my legs gave out."

Tommy helped her up, closed the lid to the toilet, and sat her down. After he reattached the shower curtain and got Morgan situated, he looked at Vickie, his brow wrinkled with concern. "Now will you go see the doctor?"

Avoiding his gaze, Vickie nodded.

The following week Vickie visited her family practitioner. "My legs have been twitching and my right one feels sort of weak."

Dr. Bowman squeezed, poked, and prodded the muscles in Vickie's legs, then picked up his clipboard and began to write.

"I know with my family history there's the possibility of Lou Gehrig's disease but I'm hoping it's Lyme disease." Vickie lifted her chin and scanned the doctor's face. When he looked up from his clipboard, she saw sadness clouding his eyes.

"I need to order some more blood work and an MRI. After that I want you to see a neurologist." He paused. "Then we'll know more."

A few weeks later, after all the tests were taken, Vickie sat in a neurologist's office with Tommy. "You're not going to tell me I have Lyme disease, are you?" she asked. She held her breath while waiting for his answer.

"No, I'm afraid not." The young doctor's face was void of emotion. "The tests indicate that you have ALS, also known as Lou Gehrig's disease. It's terminal."

His words were cold and clinical and felt like a direct hit to Vickie's heart. Tommy leaned closer to her and wrapped his arm around her shoulder. Vickie couldn't move. She sat motionless, starring at the pale yellow wall behind the doctor.

"Here's information for an organization that can help you with mobility resources and other support." The doctor handed Tommy a brochure. "Do you have any questions?"

Vickie shook her head. "No. Thank you," she said robotically. She knew what Lou Gehrig's meant. She had watched it and lived it with her dad as he died a slow and cruel death. Her thoughts involuntarily flashed back to her father, and she could see his sunken, sorrowful eyes. His perfectly functioning mind was trapped in a motionless, six foot five body in a hospital bed for the last few years of his life.

No. Please! No. A screeching alarm went off inside Vickie's head.

As they left the doctor's office, Tommy held Vickie's forearm to support her as they walked. She felt dazed, like an accident victim. They made their way to the car without a word. As they drove home, tears poured down Vickie's face. "Why? Why would God do this? Am I being punished? Did I do something wrong?"

"No, honey. You haven't done anything wrong." Tommy's voice was soft and strong.

"What are we going to do?" Choking sobs erupted from her throat. "We have children who need a mommy!" Her voice rose with each word.

Reaching over, Tommy grabbed for her hand. "It's gonna be okay. We'll get through this."

Later that night, while the kids and Tommy watched a movie, Vickie logged on the computer in the kitchen.

"What are you doing?" Tommy called to her from the couch in the family room.

"Booking a cruise."

He turned around and looked at her, his eyebrows raised. "You're what?"

"We have to build memories right now!" The urgency in her voice vibrated off the walls.

Only a few weeks later, Vickie and her family were on a Disney cruise. Each day was filled with endless delight for her three youngest children. Her older son, Patrick, loved hanging out in the game room and by the pool with other teenagers. Vickie relished every moment of her children's glee, and yet the reality of the disease lurked like a shadow. One night she awoke in a panic. "Thomas! I can't breathe!"

"What's wrong?" Tommy flipped on the light of their small cabin room.

"It's dark!"

"Honey, I just turned on the light."

"It's still dark!" Vickie grabbed Tommy's arm like he was a drowning child. "You can't leave me."

"I won't." He stroked her back.

"I feel like Satan is sitting on the edge of this bed. It's so dark." Her grip on Tommy's arm tightened. He put his hand over hers and prayed. "Don't turn off the light," she whispered when he was finished. A few minutes later, with Vickie still hanging on to him, Tommy began softly snoring. She kept her eyes open for a long time, not trusting the Darkness she knew was hiding in the shadows, eager to seize her.

As the months went by, Vickie passed through different emotional and spiritual stages. At the beginning she was all about cramming in as much living as possible. She and her family went on three different cruises and socialized as much as they could with family and friends. But as Vickie's symptoms grew worse, her anxiety attacks increased. Each time some part of her body stopped functioning, such as an arm or a leg, she had to grieve the loss, which put her on a roller coaster with anger and sadness.

"What good am I doing just sitting in my stupid red recliner all day?" she asked her Bible study group one Wednesday morning. Nine women formed a circle of chairs in a small classroom inside the church, while bright mid-morning sunlight poured through a row of windows. "What purpose could this possibly have?" Her emotions felt tossed up and down like a towel in a dryer. "My biggest fear is being useless," Vickie continued. "I watched that happen with my dad, and it looks unbearable." Vickie's thick, dark brown hair fell down around her shoulders, and other than the wheelchair she sat in, she looked young and healthy. "I keep feeling God tell me this whole journey is not about me. It's about Him and what He can do. I want my kids to see that. I don't want them to be mad or bitter at God." Vickie sighed and scanned the familiar faces looking at her.

"Why don't we pray about that," one woman suggested. The other women agreed, and they all bowed their heads. As they prayed, Vickie felt like a warm blanket was enveloping her. "Thanks." She smiled at her friends when they were finished. "I needed that."

One morning, just as summer was approaching, Vickie lay in bed pouring out her heart to God while she waited for Tommy to finish up his morning routine with the kids. Once they were off to school, he would come get her out of bed to bathe and dress her. As she waited, she pleaded with God. *You know I'm not afraid to die . . . I'm just not ready yet! There's so much left for me to teach my kids. So much left for me to do with them!* Her thoughts drifted to the upcoming summer and she closed her eyes. *Oh God, please provide people to love on my kids this summer. You know Tommy can't do it all. Please give us people who can love them and help us take care of them.*

A week later, as summer break kicked off, Vickie watched in amazement as people began to swoop in and shower her children with love and fun. There were zoo outings and pool parties; there were park adventures and popcorn movie nights; there were giggle-fest sleepovers and lazy park picnics. As Vickie experienced this outpouring of love on her kids, something inside her heart shifted.

You really will take care of them . . . won't You? she prayed one evening as she thought about how loved and happy her children were. A sweet rush of peace swept through her whole body. *You're showing me Yourself . . . You're showing me they'll be okay.* Later that night, when Tommy crawled into bed after putting the kids to bed, she turned her head—the only thing left she could move—and whispered, "You're going to be okay."

He rolled over on his side toward her. "I can't do this without you."

"You know what God is telling me?"

"What?" he asked, snuggling into her.

"That He really *will* provide." Vickie drew out the word "will," her brown eyes shining as she looked at her husband. "It's not just some Bible verse that sounds all cliché and nice. It's real! Look at how He's taken care of us financially. Look at how He's given us people to smother our kids with love."

Tommy reached up and swiped a strand of Vickie's dark hair off her cheek and tucked it behind her ear. "Mmm-hmm."

"I've been thinking that I don't want to die here at home. I don't want you or the kids to have to live with that. When the time comes, I want to go to the hospice care center and die there. You guys don't need the memory of me passing away here in this bed."

Tommy's lashes grew damp. He put his arms around his wife and whispered, "I love you."

"I love you too." She tilted her head forward as he leaned in and kissed her.

. . . .

Vickie has taught me a lot about not clinging to my life. I'm nowhere near the place and peace she is, but in a distinct way, I've gotten to taste Matthew 10:39 through her.

Both my panic attack on the boat in Peru and Vickie's panic attack on the cruise ship were because we were *clinging*. Panic comes from clinging. Clinging comes from fear. A friend of mine, going through a divorce, told me that he was clinging to his marriage—long after his wife had left him—like a man hanging on to the edge of a cliff. He described himself as holding on so tight that it was like his fingernails were digging into the cliff, scraping into the rock as he dangled. What he found out was that when he finally let go, the drop wasn't that far down. In fact, he found God was on a ledge right below him, and he barely fell at all.

> If you cling to your life, you will lose it; but if you give up your life for me, you will find it.
> MATTHEW 10:39 (NLT)

We cling, we hold on, we dig in our fingernails, and all the while Jesus whispers to us, "Let go . . . I'm here to catch you."

So how do we wake up in the morning and do this? Lose our lives to Him?

For most of us I think it's a little bit like losing weight. You don't just drop fifty pounds in one day. You lose a little each week. Slow and steady. A pound here, a pound there. Two inches in the waist, one inch in the hips. Over the past year I've watched Vickie lose herself a little at a time. A release here, a let go there. I've watched her, steeped in emotions and questions, traverse her way around mountains. Little by little, step by step, eyes on Him, she let go. She stopped clinging. She died in Him.

Vickie is not the same woman I first met a year and a half ago. She's changed. A couple of weeks ago, when I was with her last, her bedroom was so filled with serenity. I wanted to crawl underneath her pale pink sheets and lie next to her just so I could soak in the palatable peace surrounding her.

During my visit she told me about deciding to die at the care center instead of at home. A huge lump swelled up in my throat when she told me. I volunteer at the hospice center she will die in. I could picture her there on a plastic mattress with a plastic pillow. I thought about how I would hate to die there, with strangers wiping my bottom, invading my privacy. I thought about how Vickie could have told Tommy she'd like to die at home and how he would have warmly obliged. He's one of the kindest, most attentive husbands I've ever been around. I thought about how lovely it would be for her to die in her pink sheets on the queen-size bed they've shared since they were first married. She could die in her own room, surrounded by the familiar things she's collected over the years, each telling a piece of her story. She could die with privacy in the sanctuary of her own home.

When Vickie told me about her decision, my fingers stopped typing for a moment and I glimpsed it—there in front of me lay paralyzed a living color picture of a woman who had lost her life for Christ.

The Message translates Matthew 10:39, "If your first concern is to look after yourself, you'll never find yourself. But if you forget about yourself and look to me, you'll find both yourself and me."

Vickie had forgotten herself. She had looked to Christ. She had found herself. She had found Him. I could see it with my own eyes.

Losing ourselves, pound by pound, step by step, is a Christ-centered, Christ-saturated process. We are all at different places in our lives with God, and losing ourselves is going to look different for each of us. Forgiveness may be your area of losing yourself right now. Or it may be giving away something you love. Perhaps losing yourself is letting go of control in an area of your life or laying down something or someone you're holding on to. Or maybe it's speaking the truth in love to someone or admitting you were wrong.

Listen. He is whispering right now. "Come lose yourself . . . Come die with Me . . . find yourself . . . you will find Me."

. . . .

Author's Note:

I was volunteering at hospice when Vickie passed away. There is no coincidence in this. I hadn't had a volunteer shift for several weeks, and the shifts are only three hours long. Yet she died on my little three-hour shift. I got to spend time with her, sitting on her bed, feeding her water droplets through a straw. In my volunteer work I've sat bedside with many people as they were dying. But I've never experienced anything like sitting bedside with Vickie. She was conscious and communicating and gracious until just before she left this earth. Usually people are nonresponsive days or at least hours before they die. Not Vickie. She was thanking people as best she could, as it was difficult for her to talk; she was concerned about how others were doing, not wanting anyone to be put out; and she invited people into her dying—not for her sake but for the sake of others.

She died to Him on her deathbed.

I found out later that it was her wish to give her long, lush hair to an organization that makes wigs for cancer patients. After she died they cut off her beautiful hair so others could wear it.

That is so Vickie.

Reflections

♦ Jesus says, "If you give up your life for me, you will find it." What does giving up your life mean? What does finding your life mean?

_____

_____

_____

_____

_____

_____

♦ In what area of your life is God impressing you to "lose yourself"?

w/ Dayrota
w/ possission — hold loosely
w/ control — schedule — directions

♦ Read Genesis 22:1–19. Connect that story of Abraham with Jesus' words in Matthew 10:39: "Whoever finds his life will lose it, and whoever loses his life for my sake will find it."

Abraham had to be willing to lose all —
& in doing so gain all —
Abraham did give his son eventually —
Jesus!

♦ Which part of Vickie's story spoke to you the most? How so?

chosing hospice —

God wants to give you *life!*
Lose yourself to Him.

6

Praise

God can change you. Worship Him.

She came and worshiped him.

MATTHEW 15:25 (NLT)

A certain woman has captivated me for weeks now. I'm in awe of her. Every morning I read and reread her story. She has become my new mentor. My role model. Read her story below and allow me to explain my fascination.

> Then Jesus left Galilee and went north to the region of Tyre and Sidon. A Gentile woman who lived there came to him, pleading, "Have mercy on me, O Lord, Son of David! For my daughter is possessed by a demon that torments her severely."
>
> But Jesus gave her no reply, not even a word. Then his disciples urged him to send her away. "Tell her to go away," they said. "She is bothering us with all her begging."

Then Jesus said to the woman, "I was sent only to help God's lost sheep—the people of Israel."

But she came and worshiped him, pleading again, "Lord, help me!"

Jesus responded, "It isn't right to take food from the children and throw it to the dogs."

She replied, "That's true, Lord, but even dogs are allowed to eat the scraps that fall beneath their master's table."

"Dear woman," Jesus said to her, "your faith is great. Your request is granted." And her daughter was instantly healed. (Matt. 15:21–28 NLT)

First, I want to know this woman because she knows pain with a capital P. And maybe I'm a sicko, but her pain draws me toward her. I want to know more of her story and how she has survived and what she has learned. The pain she sleeps with every night is the pain of a mother. As a mother, I relate. The pain I've felt over my children is raw and bleeding—vulnerable, desperate, and visceral. A few weeks ago my youngest son almost cut off his finger in a doorjamb. When I tell the story, I grimace, holding my own finger as it begins to throb. This is the way of a mother. Reading this mother's story, I can only imagine the depths of her pain as she helplessly watches her demon-tormented daughter. Her soul-piercing, desperate-mother anguish pulls me toward her.

I think most of us, if we're honest, can relate to this pain attraction. We feel more comfortable, more normal, more secure around people who struggle. My son, when he was in fifth grade, encapsulated this sentiment once when we were in a psychologist's waiting room. We were there to talk to a counselor about his fear of sleeping alone. As we sat in the packed waiting room, he leaned over to me and whispered, "I like this place."

I scrunched my eyebrows at him. "Why?"

"Because everyone here has problems," he replied.

Isn't that the truth? We feel more comfortable around people like us—people trying to find their way. People with problems. People who know pain. People who need help—like this woman talking to Jesus.

I find myself further drawn toward this woman because of her response to the silence of God. When she first pleads with Jesus for help, He doesn't answer her. As a Jesus follower, this is a little hard to swallow. This is not the Jesus I know. Why wouldn't He answer this poor woman? To add salt to her wound, the disciples get irritated with her and ask Jesus to send her away. So here is this woman in profound emotional pain, ignored by Jesus, and unwanted by His disciples—and this is where my fascination with her peaks. Listen again to what she does: Jesus didn't answer her, "but she came and worshiped him." The disciples told her to bug off, "but she came and worshiped him." Her daughter was demon possessed, "but she came and worshiped him." She persevered through the pain of her mother's heart, the silence of Jesus, the disciples' rejection, and she found a way—through worship.

It's one thing to praise and worship God when life is peachy. But what about when God is silent? What then? What about when life falls apart? What about when depression takes hold of us or when a loved one dies? How do we keep connected to God?

I think one answer is through worship.

DeDe is a woman I met on the mission trip to Peru. She led worship for our group, and once while she was leading, she shared, "I know the power of worship because it got me through my darkest hours." When she said this, I knew I needed to learn from DeDe.

· ·

"I'm going to be up in my room," DeDe announced, pulling out chips and pretzels from the cupboard and setting them on the countertop. "Here's food if you get hungry before dinner." She glanced at

her two teenage sons, whose lanky bodies were sprawled out watching television in their family room. "Unless there's a death, do not bother me."

"'K, Mom," they grunted in unison.

As DeDe climbed the stairs to her room, desperation inside her mounted with each step. The moment she shut the door, tears sprang from her eyes. Weeping, she peeled off her work clothes and put on a pair of gray sweats. Her chest felt like an empty cavity, void of a heartbeat. She glanced at the bed and wrestled with the urge to lose herself underneath the covers like she'd been doing most nights since Blake left. *Lord, I can't keep living like this.* She felt the familiar sorrow pressing down on her. *You've got to do something, Lord!* she pleaded, her chin quivering.

Depression had clamped down on her like a suit of armor she couldn't get off. She picked up the Bible that lay on her bedside table and sat down on the edge of her bed. *Help me*, her heart cried. She tried to pray but couldn't. She stared at the Bible on her lap and thought about her double life. DeDe volunteered as the assistant youth pastor in her church, leading young people in their spiritual growth. Yet, when she was at home, apathy consumed her; she felt like a smoldering fire, dull and lifeless, smoke without fire. As her marriage had crumbled, it seemed her ability to connect with God faded. *Lord*, she persisted, *I need You to do something or I'm going to die.* She dropped her Bible on the bed, picked up a pillow, and hugged it. Waiting to feel a whisper of hope from God, she did not sense anything.

DeDe knew if she sat on her bed any longer, she'd lose the battle and crawl underneath the covers, allowing the pain to consume her. She grabbed her Bible and stood up. Flipping it open to the book of Psalms, she started to read out loud. Her toes dug into the carpet as she slowly walked back and forth in a U-shape around her bed, reading psalm after psalm. She felt like a robot going through a preprogrammed set of mechanical motions. But she kept pacing and reading anyway. She lost track of time, and it was dark before she heard a gentle knock on her door.

"Yes?"

"Mom? Nana called but I told her you were busy."

DeDe set her Bible on the bed and opened the door. Aaron, her younger son, had in the past year sprouted like a weed and was now several inches taller than her. He eyed her for a moment, then blurted, "What are we having for dinner?"

"Are you hungry?" She put on a smile for him.

"Starving."

"I'll make dinner." She hated being a mom who was emotionally checked out, so no matter how hollow she felt, she worked to shield the boys from her pain. They had already lost enough. "I'll make some burgers." She reached out and gave Aaron's arm a tender squeeze.

After dinner and doing the dishes with her sons, DeDe retreated back to her bedroom and closed the door. She crawled underneath her covers and curled up into a fetal position. Her heart squeezed as she stared at the empty spot beside her. She closed her eyes and imagined Blake lying there with her. After their sixteen years of marriage, she had memorized every part of his body. She longed for his lean arms to enfold her. Tears pooled in her eyes. *Lord, why don't You stop this divorce?*

She thought about how much Blake had changed since coming home from the hospital over a year and a half ago. He'd always been a health nut, so when he got sick and spent nearly a month in the hospital, fighting pneumonia, it had been a surprise to everyone. During that same time period, the church they'd been attending since they were first married began to unravel due to marital problems between the pastor and his wife. Adding to all of this, while Blake lay sick in a hospital bed, a good friend of theirs had been hit and killed in a car accident.

When Blake finally did come home, he was physically weak and

emotionally disengaged. He began falling asleep every night on the couch while watching television. Even when DeDe begged him to come to bed, he mumbled lame excuses, saying he'd be up later, but he never came. That had been the beginning of her sleeping alone.

He had mentally pulled away from their boys too. Finally, after many months of his withdrawal, DeDe had given him an ultimatum. As he was leaving on a business trip one morning, she stood in the doorway of their home and pronounced, "You need to decide what you want to do about this marriage . . . what you want to do about your family." She noticed as she looked into his dark eyes, waiting for him to respond, that it was like a light inside him had been shut off. He said nothing, turned, and left. Blake never returned to their home after that trip. He moved in with friends, and then got his own apartment.

DeDe's pillow grew damp with tears as her thoughts washed over the memory. *Lord, I've begged You to bring Blake home.* A sob rose up her throat. *Why, Lord, did he stop loving me?* Her whole body began to shake as she gave way to the overwhelming sadness inside her heart.

The next night when she got home from work, she told the boys once again not to disturb her. She changed into comfortable clothes, picked up her Bible, and began to pace the bedroom reading psalms aloud. Although her spirit didn't seem to shift as she read, at least she wasn't lying in bed with a pillow over her head, wishing she would just slip away.

For weeks she did this every night, reading and walking, walking and reading. One night she read Psalm 73 over and over again.

> Truly God is good to Israel,
> to those whose hearts are pure.
> But as for me, I almost lost my footing.
> My feet were slipping, and I was almost gone . . .
> My health may fail, and my spirit may grow weak,

but God remains the strength of my heart;
he is mine forever. (Ps. 73:1–2, 26 NLT)

As she read, she found herself praying for the first time in months. *Yes, Lord, You are good. I almost lost my footing, and I was almost gone but—You are my strength.*

Her prayer continued for the next several minutes, and then abruptly she stopped pacing and stared transfixed at her bedroom wall. Her mind fluttered like a bird trying to land but not finding the branch she'd been roosting on. She searched inside her heart for a moment and found that the all too familiar grip of despair wasn't as close at hand. It felt a little farther away. Fueled with hope, she continued to pace, and instead of just reading the passages, she prayed them.

"Yet I still belong to You." *Yes, Lord. I belong to You.*

"You hold my right hand." *Yes, Lord, I may not have a husband to hold my hand, but You hold my hand!*

Night after night she continued this routine. Sequestered in the sanctuary of her bedroom after work, she opened up to Psalms and read and prayed. In time, like a spring flower opening its petals after the rain, her prayers bloomed into praise. She found her thoughts refocused from the pain and pity of her circumstances to the greatness and goodness of God. The armor suit of depression unbolted piece by piece and fell off. Her bedroom became a haven of praise and worship, unhinging her from the bleak reality of her impending divorce and reconnecting her soul to God.

One evening many months after she started the prayer time in her bedroom, Blake came over to pick up the boys. He walked into the kitchen, and DeDe, chopping a head of lettuce, looked up at him. "Oh, hi." She smiled. "I think the boys are up in their rooms."

"Okay, I'll go get them."

DeDe stopped chopping and watched Blake as he left the kitchen. She was accustomed to surges of anger whenever she saw him. But

now, as she looked at him, she felt nothing. He was a different man than the one she had married. Even though they had once been best friends, she felt as if she were looking at a stranger.

A moment later the boys came bounding down the stairs. "We'll be back in a couple of hours," Blake told her, walking toward the front door. "See you later."

His voice sounded hollow to DeDe. "See you later," she said, scooping lettuce into a bowl. As DeDe stood alone in the kitchen, she became acutely aware that there was no knot in her stomach or pangs of pain in her chest. *Lord*, she prayed, as a tentative smile nudged up her face, *this is You. You're healing my heart. You're delivering me from the pain.*

She wiped her hands on a dish towel as the smile continued to creep up her cheeks. Walking into the family room, she sank down on the couch. She looked up toward the ceiling and did what she now was so accustomed to doing—praising God.

. . . .

Praise and worship are Satan's worst nightmare. They take off the chains that bind us and cause an earthquake in our souls. Look, for example, at what happened to Paul and Silas when they worshiped the Lord in prison:

> Around midnight Paul and Silas were praying and singing hymns to God, and the other prisoners were listening. Suddenly, there was a massive earthquake, and the prison was shaken to its foundations. All the doors immediately flew open, and the chains of every prisoner fell off! (Acts 16:25–26 NLT)

Who knows how long they had been praying and singing? My guess is—since it was midnight when their chains fell off—they'd been going at it for a while. DeDe, too, did not experience an immediate change in her heart and emotions when she began her bedroom walk-about. It took months of her wearing a path into her bedroom carpet every day after work. The mother in Matthew, and DeDe, did not give up. They both pushed into the pain of their realities and chose to keep engaging with God.

Praise and worship are a continued "yes" to God. We can hate our circumstances. We can feel heartbroken over a sick child or unfaithful spouse. We can detest an illness or our present state of affairs. Yet we can still nod "yes" to God through acknowledging that He is good, faithful, trustworthy, all-knowing, all-powerful, all-present, just, kind, patient, and unconditional in His love. Regardless of the condition of our lives, God is still God. And when we acknowledge this, we engage in worship.

In C. S. Lewis's book *The Lion, the Witch and the Wardrobe*, the wardrobe is a doorway into Narnia—a whole new world for the four Pevensie children. So, too, praise is a doorway into a new world for us. It is a doorway that leads to discoveries and experiences with God that are otherwise unavailable. It is a doorway that leads away from ourselves. DeDe told me how she would lose herself, her pain, her problems when she got lost in her bedroom. Instead of being gripped by a preoccupation with Blake, her whole being became focused on God.

Judith Houghton writes in her book *Transformed into Fire*, "Few things can corrupt a time of prayerful reading like specific expectations about what you need God to do for you. Such expectations subtly assert themselves as your focal point." When our eyes are wholly on Him, we are released from the binding of our circumstances, worries, and failures, and just like DeDe, we find ourselves transformed. Houghton explains this: "Attentively dwelling in the presence of God is our most potent and supreme source of transformation. We can only be transformed into God's image by focusing our gaze, our attention, to the glory of that image."

When DeDe broke through into a place of praise and worship, a

place where she was absorbed in God, she changed. Her pain was not all-consuming; her future was no longer hopeless. A steady stream of peace and joy replaced her apathy. Through worship, she found herself alive and whole once again.

My pastor, Steve, recently gave a message about worship. He talked about a Jamaican man with long dreadlocks who had attended his former church. The man would *very* actively engage in worship on Sunday mornings. When the music was upbeat, this man jumped up and down in the front row, his dreadlocks flying. When the music was a slower, more soulful tempo, the young man would lie prostrate on the ground in worship. Other churchgoers complained about the man because they felt he was distracting. Yet Steve learned a lot about praise from the young Jamaican man, including that praise and worship are not meant to be passive pursuits from half-alive people.

Praise and worship are not sit-back-and-watch-the-show activities. God repeatedly encourages us to actively praise. In the Bible, He uses verbs like dance, clap, sing, bow, bend, shout, and raise your hands to describe His people worshiping. DeDe found that pacing and reading psalms out loud kept her actively engaged in worship and prevented her from drifting into a sea of distracted thoughts and self-absorption. *How* we engage in praise is individual and unimportant. *That* we engage is the difference between connecting with God and missing out on Him completely.

> It is God who arms me with strength
> and makes my way perfect.
> 2 SAMUEL 22:33

What I learn from the pain-drenched mother in Matthew and from DeDe is that engaging in active worship is not a pastime for when life is good. Daring to praise and worship God in the midst of our failures and disappointments means our hearts and minds are intent on Him and all that He is. With our attention fixed on Him, a revolution occurs inside our souls and we *do* change.

I was drawn to write DeDe's story because I want to learn to live a life of worship. I want to step through the wardrobe door once and for all and live in a new land, unbound from myself. Eyes glued on Him. I want that revolution.

Thus, I continue my pursuit of learning how to deeply worship.

> Hear my cry, O God;
> Listen to my prayer.
> From the ends of the earth I call to you,
> I call as my heart grows faint;
> Lead me to the rock that is *higher than I.*
>
> Psalm 61:1–2 (emphasis added)

Reflections

♦ What prevents you from engaging in undistracted praise and worship?

others

Busyness

worry

ungratefulness

♦ How do you like to _actively_ praise and worship?

raise hands

dance

move

♦ Psalm 73:16–17 says, "When I tried to understand all this, it was oppressive to me till I entered the sanctuary of God; then I understood." What is in your life that you would like God's perspective on? Can you "enter His sanctuary" and worship Him over this?

♦ DeDe found it impossible to pray after her husband left. Have you ever had times in your life when you couldn't pray? What did you do?

Asked others to pray

Jadan's accident

♦ Read 2 Chronicles 20:1–30, which describes how a courageous act of praise conquered a powerful enemy. How does the passage of Scripture speak to you?

_____

_____

_____

_____

_____

♦ Psalm 22:3 says, "Yet you are holy, enthroned on the praises of Israel" (NLT). Reflect on this. What does it say to you?

You (god) are their King when you are seated on

their praises

_____

_____

_____

♦ Which part of DeDe's story spoke to you the most? How so?

she "did" something — no silent motionless

prayer

_____

_____

_____

. . . .

**God can change you.
Worship Him.**

7

Believe

**God can do anything.
Have faith in His power.**

For nothing is impossible with God.

LUKE 1:37

I've known Sandee for more than seven years now. I met her when I interviewed older, wiser women for a book I coauthored. After the interviews were over and the stories were written, I kept meeting with Sandee on a regular basis. When I'm with her, just sitting across the table from her at our favorite Mexican restaurant, I feel closer to God. She has a faith that infiltrates me. She has wisdom and experience that I can't get enough of. She picks me up like a pawn in a chess game and moves me closer to the King whenever I'm with her.

It used to be that when we had lunch I'd try to remember important things she said, filing them away in my brain. But that became too frustrating because nearly everything she said I wanted to remember. So now when we have lunch I bring my laptop (which cracks Sandee up) and type as we converse over fajitas and chimichangas. A little unorthodox, maybe, but when we're together it's like I'm a gold digger who's struck it rich. I don't want to miss a single nugget.

When Sandee was a young mother, she received a call from the "other" woman, who informed her that her husband was having an affair. Sandee did everything she could to save her marriage, but to no avail. After the divorce, she had few job options to support her two girls. She ended up having to move from her small Midwest town so she could find a job.

Many times while raising her daughters on minimum wage, she lacked the financial resources for basic things their family needed such as a car or money to pay the next utility bill. But God always found a way to meet her needs—someone would show up at her door with an envelope of money, or her church elders would give her a car that had been donated to the church. When others around her were awestruck at the ways in which God took care of her, she would always laugh and say, "I'm not surprised one bit! After all, this is *God* we're talking about."

I've listened to scores of Sandee's stories, and they leave me panting for just a smidge of her faith, just a fraction of her belief in a God of the impossible. I wish the whole world knew Sandee. The Spirit of God is so real in her it fills up any room she's in. Yet, from the world's point of view, she's a nobody. She makes an unimpressive salary as a caseworker helping needy families. She's not in the news and doesn't have a Web page or a blog. But my guess is, her life is making headlines in heaven because of the way she dares to believe—and I mean *truly believe*—in a God of the impossible.

. . . .

Sandee hung up the phone and looked across the table at her employer, Mrs. MacAllister. "That was my doctor. He says he wants me to come into his office this morning."

"Really? Well, good." Mrs. MacAllister took the last sip of coffee from her dainty gold and blue coffee cup.

"Mmm-hmm." A sliver of irritation ran through Sandee as she watched the snowflakes falling outside Mrs. MacAllister's kitchen window. She hated to drive in the snow, and besides, she had ironing to do.

"Don't you worry about today," Mrs. MacAllister said, reading Sandee's thoughts. "I didn't have much for you to do anyway." She took their coffee cups to the sink and rinsed them. "I'll drive you over there. You don't need to be driving yourself when you're not feeling well. Besides, whatever your doctor has found can't be too bad, otherwise he wouldn't let you drive yourself. Right?"

"Mmm-hmm," Sandee agreed, but she still felt bad about not getting her work done. She set her hands on top of the kitchen table as she stood. The nagging pain in her abdomen redirected her thoughts. "Well, at least maybe now I'll get some answers. I'm sick and tired of feeling so sick and tired."

Less than an hour later Sandee walked into the doctor's office. The nurse, whom Sandee had become friends with, had a line of worry creasing her brow. "You don't need to sign in." She motioned for Sandee to follow her. "Come back and I'll put you in a room. Dr. Trevar shouldn't be too long."

Sandee's bones ached and she was weak with exhaustion as she walked after the nurse.

"Have a seat." The nurse pointed to the exam table. "The doctor wants me take some more blood."

Sandee scooted onto the exam table and pushed up her right sleeve. "You guys won't stop until you have all my blood," she teased.

After the nurse left, Sandee reclined on the table and closed her eyes.

Fifteen minutes later, Dr. Trevar lightly knocked on the door.

Startled, Sandee sat up. "Goodness, I must have dozed off."

"Sorry to keep you waiting."

"Not a problem."

"Sandee, I'd like to run some more tests on you."

"Okay."

"And I'd like to admit you to the hospital where we can keep an eye on you."

Not surprised, Sandee nodded. Over the years she'd been in and out of hospitals many times due to a childhood heart condition. She suffered from hypertension and a heart valve that did not function properly. When she was a little girl, the doctors had predicted she wouldn't live through childhood, but she'd surprised everyone. The way she'd been feeling over the last few months, however, seemed unrelated to her heart issues. There was something unfamiliar about it.

"Do you want me to have a van take you over there or do you think you can walk?"

Sandee chuckled. "You don't think I can walk a few yards to the next building?" She arched her eyebrows at the doctor.

"Okay, okay. Just checking." He gave her a weak smile.

"Will you meet me over there?" Sandee asked.

"Yes. After they've admitted you, I'll be over. Your white blood cell count is what concerns me at this point." Pulling his clipboard to his chest, he added, "But we'll get to the bottom of this and figure out what's going on."

"I know you will." She gave him an appreciative nod. He'd been her doctor for many years and knew her history well. She was grateful for his committed attention to her health issues and trusted him completely.

After filling out the admission paperwork and getting settled into a third-floor hospital room, Sandee called her son, Isidro, whom she'd adopted several years earlier when he was a teenager. He had come into their home emotionally broken and needy, but Sandee had spent a lot of time and energy pouring the love of God into him and making their home a safe harbor for him.

"Hi, honey." Sandee's voice was rusty and tired. "The doctor has admitted me to the hospital to run some more tests."

"What?" She could hear the alarm in his voice. "Why?"

"Sweetie, they just need to figure out what's going on with me. It's been months of me feeling bad."

After hanging up with him, she called her oldest daughter, Charlynne, followed by a call to her youngest daughter, Shaunya. That evening they all came to the hospital armed with Sandee's personal belongings. Charlynne marched into the room with a small black suitcase. Setting it down on a chair near the radiator, she unzipped it and pulled out two nightgowns. In her left hand, she held up a powder blue gown, and in her right hand, she held up a vibrant peach gown. "Here, Mom, which one do you want to wear?"

"I think I'll go with that one tonight." Sandee pointed with obvious delight at the peach one.

Over the next week, Sandee went through relentless testing, and with each passing day, she grew weaker. One evening Dr. Trevar came to Sandee's room while her children were all there. "We've been able to identify what's making your mom so ill," he began as he clutched the clipboard in his hands against his chest. "We've found a cancerous tumor in her pancreas."

Charlynne, standing at the edge of Sandee's bed, reached down and held her mom's feet through the thin white sheet.

"Pancreatic cancer is very difficult to detect because the pancreas is tucked behind so many other organs." Dr. Trevar took a piece of paper from his clipboard and began drawing a picture of the pancreas and the organs around it. "We've taken cross-sectional X-rays of it and have been able to determine that it's about the size of a golf ball." He drew a circle on his diagram.

"What can we do to treat it?" Charlynne asked.

"Well . . ." Dr. Trevar adjusted his glasses. His intense eyes scanned Sandee's children before he spoke. "You have some decisions to make. We can go in and try to remove the tumor from your mother. However"—he hesitated, shifting his eyes toward Sandee—"your mom is very ill, and I'm not sure she can survive such an invasive procedure."

"What happens if Mom doesn't have the surgery?" probed Shaunya, who was standing near the window.

"With the surgery we estimate she would have about four months to live."

The room grew still. Isidro squeezed his mother's hand as tears leaked out of his eyes.

"Without the surgery it will be less than that," Dr. Trevar said softly. "That's the nature of pancreatic cancer. It's one of the most devastating cancers and one of the quickest."

After the doctor left, Sandee motioned her children to get on the bed. Crawling in next to her, they began to sob. A spasm of pain shot through Sandee's heart. She ached for them. Even though they were all in their twenties, she knew they still desperately wanted and needed a mom. With one hand stroking Isidro's back and the other hand interlaced with Shaunya's hand, she tried to reassure them. "Remember, you guys"—she reached over and brushed the tears off Charlynne's cheek—"this is a win-win situation. We know the Lord and we know if I go home, it's wonderful. And if I don't go, it's wonderful too. We just need to know what His attitude is in this, what He wants."

"I know what He wants!" Shaunya said, wiping her nose with a tissue. "He hates cancer."

A soft smile tugged at Sandee's cheeks. "We still need to go to Him and see what He's saying . . . is it my time or not?"

"Not!" the three agreed in unison.

During the next few days, Sandee and her children made the decision she would go ahead with the surgery. Word spread through their large church about Sandee's cancer, and church members set up a prayer vigil. Soon there were people praying twenty-four hours a day,

seven days a week. After each hour of prayer, the assigned individual was to call the hospital and see how Sandee was doing. The hospital was flooded with phone calls and visitors for Sandee. Eventually a hospital patient liaison had to get involved and limit both Sandee's phone calls and visitors.

One afternoon, a nurse was changing Sandee's IV bag when a strikingly handsome doctor walked into the room. "Hello, Mrs. Bodie. I'm Dr. Devin. I'm the surgeon who'll be operating on you in a few days."

Even in her weak condition, Sandee's humor kicked into full gear as she eyed the doctor. "Why, Dr. Devin, your mother ought to be ashamed of herself."

Flustered, the doctor blinked. "Um . . . excuse me?"

"I mean the nerve of her unleashing you into the world of women." Sandee's tired eyes twinkled with mischievousness.

Dr. Devin stood speechless for a moment, then threw his head forward and began to laugh. He laughed so hard, he grabbed both his sides. "You're such a character," he said, catching his breath, "and I just met you!"

"Yes, I know. And I'll never forget it." Sandee couldn't resist. "Can I trust you to operate on me? You look too good."

"Well, I've been given the honor, but I had no idea what an honor it would be." Dr. Devin grinned, showing off glimmering white teeth. He explained to Sandee what he would be doing during the surgery and assured her by listing his credentials and surgical experience that she was in good hands.

"That comforts me to no end," Sandee said with a smirk.

"I thought it would," he jabbed back at her with another dashing smile.

Even with her sense of humor fully intact and gobs of prayer and support, Sandee's body continued to decline rapidly, and soon she began going in and out of consciousness. Her sister, Jackie, flew into town and vigilantly stayed by her bedside.

Two days before the surgery was scheduled, Sandee's pastors, Marilyn and Wally, came to visit. Pastor Wally stood at the foot of her bed and prayed for Sandee while Pastor Marilyn stood on Sandee's left side, close to her head. As Marilyn looked down at Sandee, she noticed how gaunt her friend's face had become. "Listen to me," Marilyn said, ignoring the fact that Sandee was asleep and unresponsive. She leaned down toward Sandee's ear and began to pray for healing.

After a few minutes, Sandee's eyes fluttered, and then opened. Marilyn squeezed her hand. "Hi there, kiddo. How ya doing?"

A slow smile inched up Sandee's face. "Good," she whispered.

"Did you hear me praying for you?"

Sandee's head pitched slightly forward and then backward.

"How much did you hear?"

"Every word," Sandee murmured.

"Did you receive every word?"

"Mmm-hmm." The smile did not leave Sandee's face as her eyes closed and she drifted off again.

On the day of the surgery, Sandee's three children and sister waited anxiously as a young nurse prepared Sandee. Sandee's lids were heavy, but she was awake as the nurse changed her from her frilly nightgown into a light blue hospital gown. Then the nurse tucked Sandee's hair into a cotton hospital cap. She gave Sandee some medicine, explaining it would help her relax and be more comfortable as they continued their pre-operation procedures.

A young male technician rolled an X-ray machine into her room. "Dr. Devin has requested another image of the tumor before surgery." He pulled the bulky machine next to Sandee's bed. "They'll have these pictures in the operating room so the doctor can view the tumor before the procedure and even during if he needs to," he explained to Jackie and to Sandee's kids while he positioned the machine over Sandee's abdomen. He made adjustments, and then pushed a few buttons. "There we go," he announced. "Now it shouldn't be long until

they come and get her." He maneuvered the machine toward the door. "Good luck. I hope the surgery goes well."

For the next half an hour, they huddled around Sandee's bed, nervously waiting. Then, unexpectedly, Dr. Devin rushed into the room. He was noticeably pale and stood in his surgery scrubs at the corner of Sandee's bed. His mouth was open like he had something to say, but nothing came out. He just gaped at Sandee.

Jackie interrupted his odd behavior. "What's going on?"

Turning toward Sandee's kids, he said, "There won't be any surgery on your mom today."

"What!" Jackie shouted in hysteria. "My sister needs this surgery!"

Waving his hand, he shook his head. "No. No. I'm sorry. Let me explain. There isn't any *need* for surgery today. The X-rays we just took showed absolutely no sign of a tumor." Wide-eyed, he looked back at Sandee. "There's nothing there."

"That's impossible! There's been a mistake and you people need to fix this!" Jackie ranted.

Isidro, Charlynne, and Shaunya began jumping up and down and hugging each other, tears filling their eyes.

"Mom! God healed you!" Charlynne squeezed Sandee's hands.

"I knew He would!" Shaunya cheered.

Isidro bent down and kissed Sandee's cheek.

Although the pre-operation medicine had relaxed Sandee, she was fully coherent. "Praise You, Lord."

When Jackie finally fell silent, Dr. Devin turned back toward Sandee. "I've never seen anything like this."

Sandee's face lifted up into an easy grin as she looked into his beautiful gray-blue eyes. "Doctor, I've learned that *nothing* surprises me with the Lord."

. . . .

It's been fifteen years since Sandee's tumor miraculously disappeared and, though the doctors suspected that the cancer would return, it hasn't. In her patient file, the doctor wrote, "What was there is no longer."

Sometimes I think it would be easier to have a faith like Sandee's if I had a miracle happen to me. But the deeper truth is, I find it hard to believe that God would do for me what He did for Sandee. Some obstruction inside my heart keeps me from grasping the truth that God loves me and wants to do miracles for me.

In the gospel of Mark is the story of a blind man sitting on the side of the road, who calls out to Jesus for mercy and healing. People in the crowd around Jesus tell the blind man to be quiet and leave Jesus alone. But he persists and keeps shouting, "Jesus, Son of David, have mercy on me." Jesus stops and asks the blind man to come over to Him (Mark 10:46–52). When I picture myself as the blind man sitting by the road, my heart cannot connect with Jesus stopping for me. I may call out to Him, but He wouldn't stop—not for me. I know in my head that isn't true, but how do I get my heart to believe differently? How do I become like Sandee, expectant and trusting—open and able to receive the impossible?

My spiritual mentor, Debbie, tells me it's not something I can conjure up or try harder to have. It's a work of the Holy Spirit in my heart that moves me away from the lie that He would pass me by, and toward a place of believing and receiving that I am His beloved, valuable beyond measure. So I've learned to pray, *Lord, help me believe You would stop for me.* As He draws me into Himself, I notice, little by little, the permanent cement that once bonded the lie inside my heart is slowly crumbling. I wait, on the side of the road, for Jesus to stop—for me. I know when I get to that place, when I can receive Him stopping because I call out His name, His possibilities will become real inside my soul, just like they are for the blind man and Sandee.

> So we fix our eyes not on what is seen, but on what is unseen. For what is seen is temporary, but what is unseen is eternal.
>
> 2 CORINTHIANS 4:18

It's not like Sandee is genetically wired to have such a profound faith. Her faith started out with a simple choice to say yes to God. Then she cultivated her faith choice like a well-tended garden—watered, pruned, and fertilized. Immersing herself in Scriptures, Sandee needs God's words, her life source, just as much as the air she breathes. As she says, *she lives in the Word*; His Word is more real to her than anything she can see in this world. She is planted and grounded and rooted in an eternal frame of reference so the seen world has no hold on her. It's no wonder, then, when death came knocking on her door, she had no fear. Satan, who derails us with seen realities such as disease and death, could not get a foothold in her heart. And because Sandee is not boxed into an earthly frame of reference, nothing in her life seems impossible.

A few weeks ago, my friend Nancy had a peek inside the eternal reality where Sandee lives. Nancy's elderly mom was dying in a local hospice, and Nancy sat bedside as her mom drifted in and out of consciousness the hours before she died. Nancy described it like this:

> My mom began seeing things, and when she was conscious, she would tell us what she was seeing. One time she opened her eyes and said, "There are two staircases . . . how will I know which one to take?" I held her hand and told her she would know when the time came.
>
> Sitting with her and watching this was like seeing a portal into an eternal realm. A reality I couldn't see but I knew was right there.

Even though the portal is right there, and we acknowledge the existence of an unseen heavenly world, we tend to get consumed by our seen and very real circumstances: finances, health problems, relational stresses, broken promises, loneliness, spousal disconnect, disappointments. What I learn from Sandee is to stop and redirect myself toward the unseen. When I asked her what she felt when she found out she had four months to live, she explained that when hard things happen, she goes inside herself and centers her thoughts and attention on the Lord God Almighty. She becomes focused and is reminded of His near and present reality filled with impossibilities made possible because He *is* Almighty. God is bigger, stronger, and more powerful than anything we can see.

But do we come to Him as the Almighty? I know I don't. Or at least I vacillate, wanting desperately for His almightiness over my life but not approaching it. Not really putting myself out there. Not really believing He will show up and heal me. Partially, I don't want to be disappointed, so I have a disconnect with approaching God as the Almighty. It takes abandonment to engage with God as the Almighty, and I'm not good at abandoning myself. When I read the story about the blind man on the side of the road (Mark 10:46–52), I soak in how he abandons himself, calling out to Jesus for mercy, unconcerned that he's embarrassing and irritating people around him. He just keeps hollering for Jesus, all-abandoned-like to the Almighty.

Sandee has an abandoned faith, ready and waiting to receive from God Almighty, just like the blind man. I think this is why I'm so drawn to her. When she had cancer, she knew whether she lived or died that God would do for her what she needed to have done. She did not expect God to heal her; she just wasn't surprised by it. For her, whether it was in life or death, He would make the impossible her reality. A tumor that disappears or a faith that doesn't flinch—which is more impossible? And she knew whatever the outcome, whatever

God had in mind—dancing in heaven or healed on earth, it would bring Christ glory.

I picture Sandee when I read the story in the book of Acts where Peter heals a lame man (3:1–16). He turns to the gawking people who saw the miracle and asks, "Why does this surprise you?" Basically he was saying, "People, get a clue. This has nothing to do with me. This is *God* we're talking about!" I'm sure if Sandee had been standing in that crowd, she wouldn't have been surprised at all. She would have smiled and nodded knowingly. "Indeed! People, why is this so surprising?"

Reflections

♦ Jesus said, "Which is easier: to say, 'Your sins are forgiven,' or to say, 'Get up and walk'?" (Matt. 9:5). We are wowed at physical healing, but Jesus implies a miracle occurs every time our sins are forgiven. What are your thoughts about this?

_____

_____

_____

_____

♦ Are you hesitant or eager and ready to believe that God can do anything in your life?

_____

_____

_____

_____

♦ Often miracles that we pray for don't occur, yet even though God doesn't change circumstances, He changes us through them. Can you think of a situation in your life where God has changed you though He didn't answer your prayer as you expected?

_____

_____

_____

_____

_____

_____

_____

♦ What are your thoughts on modern-day miracles? For a great discussion or for individual reflection, listen to a twenty-minute podcast available at http://www.shoutsofjoyministries.com/events/audio/2008-05-28_Joie_At_FCC_64kbps.wma. After listening, record your reactions.

_____

_____

_____

_____

_____

_____

_____

♦ Jesus said to His disciples that through faith in God, they could move mountains (Mark 11:22–24). How can you apply that to your life?

_____

_____

_____

_____

_____

_____

_____

♦ Which part of Sandee's story spoke to you the most? How so?

_____

_____

_____

_____

_____

**God can do anything.
Have faith in His power.**

8

Pray

God will answer you.
Keep talking to Him.

I will call to you, for you will answer me.
PSALM 86:7

My oldest son, Travis, was born right before I turned thirty. I was in major career mode in my twenties, and as the thirty-year mile marker came into view, I shrugged and thought, *I guess it's time to start a family.* And that was that. Nine months later I was a mom. I know, sickening to those who struggle with infertility issues. I wasn't the type of gal who was hyper-focused on becoming a mom her whole life, but when I did think about it, I always pictured myself as a mom of boys. Maybe it was because I was a tomboy growing up. Maybe it was because I never could relate to girly-girls. So when the ultrasound revealed that Travis was indeed a boy, I smiled with relief, knowing God agreed with me—I was to be a mother of boys.

The second time I got pregnant, Bruce and I decided we'd wait until the birth to confirm our baby's gender. But I knew it was a boy.

I was induced on my due date and several hours later our second baby boy came forth into the world. I'll never forget when my doctor laid him on my chest and said, "Mr. and Mrs. Greiner, you are the proud parents of a baby *girl!*"

What? a voice inside my head shrieked. *A girl? That can't be right. I'm a mother of boys!*

A few nights later, when we were home from the hospital, I dragged myself into our family room and crumpled onto the couch next to Bruce.

"What's wrong?"

Tears welled up in my eyes. "Why would God give me a girl?" My voice was garbled with emotion. "I prayed about this! I asked for boys!" I croaked, "I'm going to totally mess this up."

Bruce wrapped his arm around me, reassuring me I'd be a great mom of a girl. But in my mind, God had blown it. He had ignored my prayers and now some poor girl-child we'd given the name Jenna was going to be ruined.

Jenna is eleven years old now—and not a day goes by that I do not want to drop to my knees and thank God for giving me a little girl. She is this beautiful, creative, feminine, intelligent person who adds an imaginative, relational, thought-provoking dynamic to our otherwise boy-child family. A year later, God gave us a great surprise we named Andrew Jeffery.

What I know now that I didn't know when Jenna was born is that God didn't ignore my prayer to have boys. He did answer me. But His answer was a resounding no.

I've learned and am still learning that God's answers to our prayers are rarely what we anticipate, and often not what we hope for. But that doesn't mean He's watching us from a distance or ignoring us or just being rude.

One Sunday morning, Matt, the youth pastor at our former church, preached about God's answer to an eight-month-long prayer he'd been praying. It's a story that gives a taste of how intimately involved God is in our lives. Yet He is unpredictable. Just when you think He's not listening to you, or at least He has more important things to do—WHAMO! He tells the universe to wait, He bends down from His throne on high, and He reveals how actively He is listening.

. . . .

Matt loved his job as the junior high pastor at Rocky Mountain Christian Church. Working with teenagers made him excited to go to work every day. When the church leadership asked him to consider becoming the campus pastor for a large satellite church that was being built, Matt had mixed feelings. A part of him felt honored and eager for the opportunity, yet another part of him felt resistant and uneasy about leaving a job he loved so much.

For months Matt and his wife, Rachael, prayed about the decision, but they never felt God's direction on the issue. One night as Matt tossed and turned in bed, he kept thinking about what Scott, an elder at his church, had told him several months earlier. They had been at a conference together, and after a worship service, Scott came looking for Matt. "I just had the strangest thing happen to me," Scott said, his brow furrowed.

"What?"

"I'm not one of those people who goes around saying 'God told me to tell you something,' but during that whole worship service, I kept getting this overwhelming impression that God wanted me to tell you something, Matt."

"Really?" Matt's curiosity leaped.

"He wanted me to tell you He loves you very much and . . . " Scott paused.

"Yes?" Matt's anticipation rose like the temperature inside a convection oven.

"And if you will seek His face, He will do amazing things with your life."

Now, as Matt lay in bed with his eyes wide open, he thought about how Scott's words had been like an arrow hitting the bull's-eye of his heart. Flipping onto his side, he kicked the sheets off his legs. *God, I'm trying to seek You . . . I'll go where You want me to go, do whatever You want me to do. Just please show me.*

The following night, for what seemed like the millionth time, Matt and Rachael talked over the pros and cons of taking the new job. "I feel so conflicted." Matt pushed his half-eaten spaghetti dinner away and leaned back in his chair.

Rachael's eyes brimmed with empathy.

"You know what?" Matt said, slapping his hands on the kitchen table. "I think I need to go up to the mountains and pray until God gives me an answer."

Rachael nodded. "That's a good idea."

"I'm not going to leave until I get an answer!" Matt picked up his glass and chugged his water. "If I don't get an answer on Friday, I'm going back on Saturday. And if I don't get an answer Saturday, I'm going back on Monday. I'll keep going 'til I get an answer."

Early that Friday morning, Matt gathered up his Bible, journal, hiking boots, and a fleece sweater. It was a mild winter day and he figured he wouldn't need much. He drove an hour to Estes Park and stopped at a coffee shop before taking off on his expedition. He ordered an Americano, found a table next to a window, and pulled out his journal.

Taking a sip of his coffee, he gazed out at the bright blue sky dotted with puffy cotton-ball clouds. *God, I need You to tell me what to do.* He exhaled a long breath. Opening his journal, he began to write. *God, I absolutely love working with these teens at this church.* He set his pen down and looked again at the sky. Inside his head, a voice whispered, "What is it you love?"

I love how they don't put chains on You. I love how they assume You can do big things because You're a big God!

For several minutes Matt mulled over this idea. Yet he still felt stuck so he continued to write down his questions to God. After an hour, he slammed his journal shut. *I've been trying to figure it out on paper for eight months! I'm not getting anywhere. I just need to hear from You!*

He picked up his things and headed for his car. He drove to the entrance of the national park and paid for a pass. "I'm going to hike up past Bear Lake. Do you know how much snow is up there?" he asked the park attendant.

"Fifty feet."

"Wow! Fifteen feet. That's a lot!"

"*Fifty* feet!" A flash of humor crossed the park attendant's face as she handed Matt a park map.

"Oooh. Man. Fifty feet! That's incredible."

He found a parking spot close to the trailhead. Intimidation pricked him when he saw other hikers holding GPS gadgets, buckling on fancy snowshoes, and pulling on Gore-Tex outerwear. *Hmm, I guess it's just me, my fleece sweater, and You, God*, he thought with a smirk.

As he started out on the trail, he made sure to stay inside the snowshoe tracks. Matt walked and talked out loud to God for a long time. Then he noticed that a man and woman hiking ahead of him looked backward.

They probably think I'm nuts talking to myself. He sped up to pass them. Breathing heavily, he couldn't help but notice they looked like they belonged on the front cover of an outdoor magazine with their neon yellow and silver snowshoes and matching apparel. He waited until they were out of earshot, and then continued his dialogue with God. "Those hikers know exactly what they're doing and where they're going." He rounded a bend in the trail. "But I don't have a clue." Anxiety bubbled up inside him like carbonated soda. "God, what if I get lost in this new position?" he asked as he approached a cluster of evergreen

trees where the trail forked. Stopping, he looked around and realized he'd passed this same cluster of trees a short while ago, which meant he'd walked in a circle.

"See, God! I'm going in circles! What if I take the new position but I have no idea what I'm doing?" Matt's anxiety intensified like pressure in the cabin of an airplane. But inside his heart, a clear and distinct voice spoke: *I am the Good Shepherd. My sheep know My voice and they follow Me. I lead them into green pasture.*

"Okay . . . okay . . ." Matt exhaled, and steam puffed from his mouth. "You'll lead me."

As he trudged through the snow, he continued to talk to God, laying out all of his concerns and worries. Each time he set forth new reasons why this job might be a bad decision, the voice inside his heart spoke back, reassuring him. As Matt made his way up a steep incline, he suddenly came to a stop. "But God, what if they knew the real me . . . the me who is so unimpressive, so imperfect? They wouldn't want me for this job."

I want you, Matt.

"But, God, it's not that easy," he protested. "What if I fail? What if I blow it huge?" Matt started walking again, making his way across a rock-filled ravine. About halfway through the ravine, his left foot slipped and became wedged between two rocks. He took a step to steady himself, but his free foot plunged down into snow until he was covered up to his waist. As he stood there in a compromising position, he thought about the conversation he had with his sister the night before. "Don't get eaten by a bear or a mountain lion while you're up there," she had warned. His mind rewound some more to a television program he'd seen about a guy who was hiking around the Redwood Forest and was killed by a mountain lion.

Oh great. Matt's heart pounded as he glanced around for predators. Yanking on his snow-covered leg, he suddenly thought of 1 Peter 5:8: *Your enemy the devil prowls around like a roaring lion looking for someone to devour.* Glancing over his shoulders, he pulled his right foot out of the deep snow and worked on dislodging his other foot. His mind swirled around the thought of Satan trying to devour him as he made this job decision. Certainly if he did take the new job, Satan would be ready to pounce. Tugging his left boot free, he took another quick look over his shoulder to make sure mountain lions weren't stalking him, then hurried across the ravine.

After a while he ran into a group of hikers. "Excuse me," he interrupted their conversation, "how far until Lake Hiyaha?"

The hikers looked at him and started laughing. They turned Matt in a different direction and pointed to a crest far in the distance. "Lake Hiyaha is up there."

"Oh." Matt looked at the trail he was on. "What's up here?" He pointed.

"Lake Emerald."

"Thanks." Once the hikers were out of earshot, he exclaimed, "See, God!" Agitation crawled up his throat. "I'm headed in the wrong direction! I don't know the first thing about doing this new job."

Matt, is this you doing this or is it Me?

"You're right." He rubbed his forehead. "It's You."

As Matt walked on, a quiet stillness overcame him. Peace trickled into the cracks made by questions and doubts in his heart. The direction he'd so desperately searched for finally found him. His shoulders fell and everything in him relaxed. With a wave of relief, he proclaimed, "Okay, God. I guess You want me to be the new campus pastor." As he hiked around a bend, a small bird flew right in front of him and landed in an evergreen tree to the left of the trail. He stopped and watched. He loved wildlife and hadn't seen any, not even a bug, since he began his trek. The small tan and white bird sat perched on a branch, picking at the tree with its tiny beak. Matt stood still, soaking in its busy little movements.

As he stood there, a need rose up in him like a balloon filling with helium. Before he could stop himself, he blurted out, "God . . . if

everything I've felt has been from You today, I need You to do something. If You are here . . . and You want me to take this job . . . then I need"—he paused and drew in a deep breath—"I need that bird to come out of the tree and land on my arm." With his eyes locked on the bird, Matt raised his left arm out to the side of his body.

In the next instant the bird flew out of the tree, straight toward Matt, and landed on his outstretched arm. Holding his breath, Matt looked at the bird. The bird cocked its tiny head and gazed directly back at Matt as if saying, "Got it now?" Then the bird opened its wings and flew back to the tree.

Matt's heart thumped wildly. He looked around, hoping to find witnesses to what had just happened. He wanted to scream, "Did anyone see that?" He looked back at the bird fidgeting in the tree and was tempted to lift up his left arm and ask God to do it again. But instead, he threw back his head and started laughing. "Okay, God! I've got my answer."

Hiking down the trail toward his car, he dug his cell phone from his pocket and called his wife. "Honey! We have to talk!"

"Did God give you an answer?"

"I'd say so!"

· ·

This story is not about a young man who gets to hear from God in special ways. Or a man who somehow has more favor with God than you and me. The fact is, Matt pleaded with God for an answer for many months until he got one. There are countless stories of people who've prayed for years before God answered their prayers. And there are just as many stories like my own Jenna story, when the issue isn't time but that God doesn't give the answer we want. No, this is not a story about Matt. This is a story about God and how He *is* listening to you and me. He *does* answer.

> I call on you, O God, for you will answer me.
> PSALM 17:6

Just like a parent answers with many different responses to a child's request—yes, no, maybe later, not now, we'll see—God's answers to our prayers are wide in variety. But often when we don't get the answer we want when we want it, we lapse into assuming He's not listening. With our own agendas, we set out to get the outcome *we* want.

At the end of the movie *Prince Caspian*, Peter says to Lucy, "It's all right, Lu. It's not how I thought it would be but it's all right. One day you'll see too." I'm discovering this is often like my life of prayer with God: His answers many times aren't what I think they will be or want them to be, but in time, if I sink into God, I agree with Peter—it's okay. *If I stay in Him*, it's okay. It's when I exit Him, allowing my eyes to frantically take in the scene around me, that I begin to sink.

We have a couple of choices as we offer our petitions to God: 1) we trust His answers and wait on Him; 2) we fight His answers and force the desired outcome of our own agenda. I tend to be impatient, so it's been a long, hard road for me to learn how to set down my agenda and wait for God's answer—and accept it, even when I don't like it.

I heard about a woman who had breast cancer and underwent a mastectomy followed by long periods of radiation and chemotherapy. Just when her chemo regimen was over, cancer was found in her other breast, requiring more surgery and chemotherapy. Several years later, as sort of a celebration of her being alive, she signed up to run in a race. She got up early the morning of the race, got ready, and headed to the starting point. When the race began, she felt exhilarated. Somewhere during the second or third mile, though, she realized something was wrong. After reading race signs and listening

to other racers talk, it occurred to her she was in the wrong race! This was not the race she'd signed up for! Instead of stopping, she made a decision in that moment to keep running, saying to herself, "Well, this isn't the race I signed up for, but this is the race I'm in and I'm going to finish it."

Many times, don't we feel the same way? *God, this is not what I signed up for; this is not what I asked for.* But can we learn from this woman? Can we learn to say, *Okay, God, like it or not, this is the race I'm in. Like it or not, this is the answer You've given me. Like it or not, I'm finishing well.*

Right now I feel like I'm in the middle of a race I didn't sign up for. I refer to it as a desert. We've been trying to sell our house for what seems like forever because, after much prayer and affirmation from God, we moved our kids to a new school across town, forty minutes away. We found a church near the school, and my husband took a new job over there. The problem is, we put our house on the market right before the bottom dropped out of the economy. We long for God to replant us. To move us. We feel like disconnected nomads, driving many hours a day to and from school and school activities, not really living here, not really belonging there. I hate our nomadic existence. Why doesn't God answer our prayers? Is selling our home such a difficult request? Didn't He lead us over there in the first place? After all, we prayed a lot about this. Did we not hear Him correctly? Or is there a sinful condition in my heart He wants me to see?

I don't know. But I do know a couple of things. First, I know that this time in the desert has changed me. God has drawn me to Himself in a way I've never experienced before. It has been a tender, intimate time where He has shown me how places in my heart have been shut off from Him. He has shown me how much more He can give and how much more He wants. He has shown me He is jealous for me and delighted in me, and that He won't stop until my whole heart is truly His. And perhaps it is only in this desert place that I could hear Him whispering these things to me. I'm not sure. But I am sure I like who I am now more than I was before my time in the desert place.

Second, I've learned that when it comes to experiencing the difficulties of unanswered prayer, I am not alone. Henri Nouwen, one of my all-time favorite authors, writes, "I experience a deep sorrow . . . that the God to whom I have prayed so much has not given me what I have most desired." Nouwen is in good company with the apostle Paul, who wrote about an affliction he identified as "a thorn in my flesh": "Three times I pleaded with the Lord to take it away from me" (2 Cor. 12:7–8), but God did not take it away. God's answer was no.

We wonder why He says no to such requests.

Yet, every time I try to figure out the "whys" of God's answers, I find myself running down rabbit trails that lead nowhere. I become immersed in the here and now and what makes sense to me. And then I become despondent and discouraged. We need to remind ourselves that there will always be mystery with God. We cannot reduce His method of answering our petitions into a tidy formula or PowerPoint presentation. Unexplained answers are part of our relationship with Him. I find the further my heart is drawn into Him, the more settled my soul becomes with His answers, especially those I don't particularly care for. When my circumstances remain the same and I come to Him empty and upside down, He changes me. He sets me back on my feet and renews my strength, at least for one more day.

It's so important for us to know that even when our prayers feel like they're hitting the ceiling, that doesn't mean He isn't listening, or He is uninvolved and unconcerned with the cries of our hearts. Matt's story is a vivid reminder that God *is* indeed listening. Whether we like His answers or not, He is intimately engaged and connected to us. Do we dare to invite, accept, and trust His answers, His timing, His Godness into all the corners and spaces of our lives, like it or not?

Truth Dare

Reflections

♦ What is your biggest struggle with prayer?

Taking time to do it — getting focused

♦ List how you have experienced God answering your prayers over the past year (yes, no, not yet, maybe).

Jordan — yes

Kota — wait & see

♦ Check the activities that help you pray. Add to the list.
- ✓ Journaling
- ✓ Praying ~~as you read~~ the Bible
- ___ Reciting a written prayer (e.g., the Lord's Prayer)
- ___ Visualizing (some people find it helpful to visualize themselves talking to Jesus)
- ✓ Getting away (like Matt going up the mountains)
- ___ Reading a daily devotional
- ___ Being outside
- ___ Doing a specific activity (i.e., painting)
- — *Talk in normal conversation*
- ___

♦ How do you answer the age-old question, "Why pray?" Consider these verses:

"He will call upon me, and I will answer him; I will be with him in trouble, I will deliver him and honor him." —Psalm 91:15

"The LORD detests the sacrifice of the wicked, but the prayer of the upright pleases him." —Proverbs 15:8

"God, who has called you into fellowship with his Son Jesus Christ our Lord, is faithful." —1 Corinthians 1:9

Because this is a relationship – it takes effort/work

♦ How does the following poem on prayer speak to you?

The potency of prayer hath
subdued the strength of fire;
it hath bridled the rage of lions,
hushed anarchy to rest,
extinguished wars,
appeased the elements,
expelled demons,

burst the chains of death,
expanded the gates of heaven,
assuaged diseases,
repelled frauds,
rescued cities from destruction,
stayed the sun in its course, and
arrested the progress of the thunderbolt.

Chrysostom, c. 347–407

♦ Which part of Matt's story spoke to you the most? How so?

His passion to get God's answer — even though he didn't think it was what he wanted.

. . . .

**God will answer you.
Keep talking to Him.**

9

Breathe

God is good. Trust in Him.

No one is good—except God alone.
MARK 10:18

I've had asthma since I was three years old. And I'm not the occasional asthmatic. Asthma is a defining part of who I am. Everywhere I go I bring an inhaler—or *wheezer* as I call it. The first thing on my "did I forget anything" checklist is always my wheezer. Without it, I'm in bad shape.

Fortunately the severe asthma attacks I had as a kid are long behind me. As a child, before the invention of inhaled steroids, I was rushed to the hospital more times than I wish to remember. An asthma attack feels like slowly suffocating to death. You simply cannot get enough oxygen into your lungs. "Attack" is a great word to describe what happens to asthmatics when our lungs close up. It's a fierce battle between the malfunctioning lungs and the rest of the body. During an attack, my whole body would launch into fight mode. Sitting erect in bed, I would press my palms down on either side of me as my warfare position. My arms would be straight and taut, pushing my shoulders upward. The muscles in my back would be wound tight, their own little band of soldiers battling against the enemy. The harder it was to breathe, the harder I would fight, every fiber of my body working to pull oxygen into my lungs. After the attack was over, when medicines had finally taken effect, my back and torso were always sore for days from battle fatigue.

Here's the interesting thing—every time I was in an emergency room fighting for the next breath, invariably the doctor or nurse treating me would say, "Try and relax." Thinking back on those words, I want to slap those doctors and nurses or at least scream at the top of my lungs, "*You try and relax!*"

What a joke. Relax in the middle of an asthma attack.

Sometimes I think accepting God's sovereignty and goodness is like having an asthma attack. Everything in us launches into fight mode. We yell and kick and scream, fighting to understand, to make sense, to find the happy ending that seems right and good. And all the verses in the Bible that talk about trusting God and His plan seem like a cruel, ridiculous joke.

I'm in the constant process of learning how to accept God's sovereignty. It's a gradual evolution in my soul like a grain of sand inside an oyster slowly transforming into a pearl. As I've journeyed with God, my trust in Him has often been profoundly inspired by watching and learning from others. Recently I learned a lot about the smaller, finer details of trusting God from a man named Mike.

. . . .

After eating breakfast, Mike walked across camp to the office trailer to check his e-mail. He'd spent the better part of the past three years as a construction engineer in Iraq, helping build power plants and other projects for the ravaged country. He lived in different camp

compounds depending on the project he was working on. In Iraq he felt like his work was making a difference, helping a country that had suffered so much. While it felt good to make a difference, he deeply missed his wife, Wendy, and their three children. He got to see them about every three months, but he knew they couldn't live this way much longer.

Mike opened the trailer door and sauntered over to his laptop. When he logged in, he noticed a flashing icon letting him know he had an instant message.

"Are you up yet? I need you to call me this morning before you leave. Call me on my cell phone, sweetie. I love you."

Mike's brow creased as he noticed the message was two hours old. That meant Wendy had sent it late on Sunday night. *That's weird*, he thought, rereading the message. *Why would she want me to call her cell phone so late on a school night?*

Pulling his cell phone from the case clipped to his belt, he got up and walked outside, punching in the country code and Wendy's cell phone number. He usually had to try a half dozen times before he could connect with Wendy, but this time he got through on the first try.

"Hello." Wendy answered the phone in her usual cheerful voice.

"Hi, hon."

"Hi, sweetie. Are you getting ready to leave for Baghdad?"

"Yep. We'll leave in a few hours."

Wendy asked a few more questions, but something in her tone sounded off. Something didn't feel right. "Where are you?" Mike asked.

"I'm at the hospital," Wendy's voice grew quieter. "They just ran a CAT scan and found a tumor."

Everything seemed to freeze. "I . . . I need to get home . . ." He felt his words hit a logjam in his throat. "I'm coming home."

"No. Just stay there," Wendy said in her ever-supportive way with

him. "It's okay. It's no big deal. They're going to run some more tests . . . just wait."

"When will they know more?"

"After an MRI in the morning. Honey, just stay there until we know more."

Mike stared down at the dirt ground. An urgency swelled inside him. He needed to be with his wife. He needed to get home. They talked for a while longer and agreed to talk again as soon as she was out of the MRI.

Mike's legs were like stiff boards as he went to find his boss. His boss helped him make arrangements so he could leave immediately for home. As Mike packed his belongings, he fought the panic that threatened to consume him. *God, please get me home quickly.*

A few hours later he boarded a plane to Kuwait. When he got off the plane, he called Wendy.

"Hello." Her cheerful tone sounded forced.

"Did you have the MRI?"

"Mmm-hmm. The tumor's a bad one. They don't know for sure what type of cancer it is, but it's stage three, maybe even stage four."

Mike's heart plunged. He opened his mouth to speak but nothing came out.

"You might want to make arrangements to come home." Wendy's voice was strong and steady.

"I'm in Kuwait and getting on a plane in just a few minutes. I'll be home in twenty-eight hours."

"It's going to be okay, honey. Whatever God has in store, that's the way it's going to be."

He could feel Wendy give him an encouraging smile through the receiver, and he nodded. His wife's strength didn't surprise him. That's who she was. She was going to fight it. She was going to trust God. She was going to give to others and live well, tumor or no tumor—that's who she was.

He leaned back against a wall. "Wen, I'll be home in just a little bit. I love you."

"I love you too. It's going to be okay."

After they hung up, Mike floated on his wife's hope and courage for a minute but then a sinking helplessness weighed down on him. He dropped into an empty airport chair and stared blankly at the people passing by him.

On the long journey home, Mike felt for the first time in his life utterly out of control. He was an orderly guy who found comfort in predicting and estimating the future. He operated in an organized, systematic, and well-planned world. As he looked out the oval airplane window into the dark sky, a trembling rose from inside him. *What if . . . ?* He squeezed his eyes shut and didn't let the thought go any further. *Wendy's strong. She can beat this.* But even as he clung to positive thoughts as to a life preserver, he realized control over his life and future was a fading mirage.

When Mike finally arrived home, he and Wendy began the exhausting process of talking with dozens of specialists to find the best course of action for Wendy. After much discussion, prayer, and research, they decided to fly to Duke University, where Dr. Allan Friedman, the "Michael Jordan" of brain cancer, held his practice. They scheduled the earliest time they could get with him and flew to North Carolina a few weeks later. During those in-between weeks, Mike continued to wrestle with his lack of control over the situation.

One night he lay in bed unable to sleep. *Why is this happening?* He looked over at Wendy who was sound asleep. *Why is Wendy the one who has to go through this? This was not supposed to happen to us—we were supposed to lead normal lives . . . raise our children . . . die of old age.* Mike rolled from his side to his back and stared at the ceiling. As he lay there, his mind reeled like a bumper car bouncing off walls and spinning around.

The agony of not knowing what God had in store ate at him. "Why?

Why would You allow this?" Mike whispered as anger began to brew. "Why would a good God allow this?" He swallowed. "Are You really good? Or are You just sitting up there on Your throne, dispensing distorted justice for entertainment?" Mike looked over at Wendy again. His throat thickened with emotion. She was so beautiful to him. He knew she believed God's heart was good. "That's the ultimate question, isn't it?" He looked up at the ceiling again. "If Your heart is good?" Fatigue washed over Mike and he closed his eyes. He felt as if a heavy stone were pressing on his chest. He knew he had to answer that question: *Is God good?* He wrestled with it through the long, dark hours of the night.

Finally, his mind burning with exhaustion, he sank to the bottom of the deep pit of emptiness inside of him and whispered, "Yes." Tears burned in his eyes. "I believe Your heart is good." He opened his eyes as a surge of relief poured over him. "You are good." Scooting closer to Wendy, he wrapped his arm around her and fell asleep.

Once they were in North Carolina, Dr. Friedman ordered numerous tests and scans. After the results came in, he met with Wendy and Mike to let them know what they could expect.

"We won't really know exactly what we're dealing with until we get in there," Dr. Friedman said, his eyes moving back and forth between Mike and Wendy. "But you need to know there are serious risks associated with this kind of brain cancer. Depending on where the tumor is, there's a possibility of Wendy losing her use of speech. There's the risk of eyesight damage or total loss of vision. There's a risk of hearing damage and motor function . . ."

Mike's chest grew tight as the doctor continued down the extensive list of possible risks. He tried to concentrate on all Dr. Friedman was saying but the words began to blend together.

"And of course there's always the possibility of death." Dr. Friedman closed the file in his hand.

Panic shot through Mike's body. He nodded his head and politely thanked the doctor, but his insides were being crushed by the reality, once again, that he was not in control. Silently he repeated over and over again, *God, You are in control. You are good. I trust You*—a prayer that had become his hourly mantra.

The next day Wendy was in surgery for five and a half hours. When Dr. Friedman came out, he told Mike and the rest of the family that the surgery went well. When Wendy woke up, she was alert and talking, and Mike's whole body relaxed when he saw that she had not lost any of her abilities. Mike and Wendy flew home a week after the surgery, and Wendy began a series of chemo and radiation treatments. Several weeks after the treatments, the doctors ordered another MRI for Wendy.

When Mike got home that afternoon, Wendy's face was taut and pale. "What's wrong?" he asked, crossing the kitchen to where she stood.

"It's back." Sorrow smothered her voice.

"What do you mean?"

"I saw the MRI picture. The tumor is back. I could see it." Wendy walked into the living room and sank into the couch.

Mike followed her. *This can't be happening.* "Are you sure?"

"It looked just like the first MRI where the tumor was." Tears rolled down her cheeks.

Mike's whole body went numb. *Lord, help.* He wrapped his arms around his wife and tears began to pool in his eyes, spilling onto Wendy's shirt.

"I just had surgery eight weeks ago," Wendy choked.

He clung harder to her. A dull ache filled his stomach. "I know."

Mike and Wendy held each other for a long time. The pain in Mike's stomach moved to his chest and grew stronger with each passing moment. He wanted to fix it. To rescue her. To rescue himself. But he couldn't. "Wen," he put his nose into her hair and inhaled. "I love you."

After a while Wendy pulled away from Mike. "You still should take the boys fishing this weekend. They need that."

"No. I can't."

"Yes. You need to." She wiped her eyes with the back of her sleeve and grabbed Mike's hands. "Hon, if this is what God has and this is what it's going to be, then this is the way it's going to be. He's in control."

Moved by his wife's strength and trust, he gave her a nod.

"Let's pray."

Wendy and Mike moved from the couch to their knees. "God, I don't like this situation," Wendy began. "I don't like what's happening, but if this is what You want, I trust in that."

Mike continued, "God, I know You are there. I know You are good. I know You're going to work this out. I don't like this either, but we're going to follow You."

When they sat back up on the couch, the intense pain in Mike's chest began to dissolve. He looked at Wendy, and a sense of calmness wrapped him like a blanket. "Maybe I'll take the boys this weekend, but we'll stay one night instead of two."

Wendy smiled at him, and his heart fluttered. "I love you so much." He reached for her hand and squeezed it.

"I love you too."

The next day the doctor called and told Wendy everything on the MRI looked good. When she asked him about the big white spot on the MRI picture, he explained it was scar tissue. Mike's heart soared when Wendy told him the good news.

I wish this story had a different ending, but less than a year later, the tumor did come back. Wendy died a few weeks after it returned. Mike continues to force himself to repeat his daily prayer mantra and fall to his knees in prayer. He wrestles every day with God and the issue of control and the loss of the woman he loved. But each time he gives himself to God, he finds a little more oxygen for the next breath.

. . . .

I knew Wendy. She was my daughter's Girl Scout leader. I went to her memorial service, and the whole sanctuary was filled with bright splashes of pink because she had requested people wear pink instead of black. Mike wrote a poem for the service and in the poem he said, "Her smile could launch a thousand ships." You know what? It really could. She had this great big, beautiful smile.

Since my kids have been in school—which has been about ten years now—I've been to three funerals for mothers of young children. There's something profoundly wrong with a young child sitting at her mother's funeral. Each time I've been at one, I've wanted to stand up, stop the world, and give the child her mother back. But each time I'm left with a heart full of sorrow and a desperate plea with God to let me live until my children are grown.

So how do we proceed as Christians with a good God who allows mothers to be taken from their children? How do we accept God's plan when we hate it? How do we come to terms with His control over everything? I don't know. My three-and-a-half-pound brain cannot wrap itself around that part of God. But every time I wrestle with these sorts of questions, the image that pops into my mind is a meandering dirt road that comes to a fork. I picture myself walking down that road and getting to the fork. Which way am I going to go? North or south?

Here's where my thoughts take me: in the end, God is the only real hope I have. At the end of the day, He's the only thing I cannot lose. I could lose the use of my body like Vickie did. I could lose my sister like Jennifer did. I could lose my marriage like DeDe did. But I can't lose Him. He's the only thing I have that I can never, ever lose. So I have to go to the north. I have to choose Him. Even when I hate His plan.

> Draw near to God and He will draw near to you.
>
> JAMES 4:8 (NASB)

The doctors and nurses told me to relax in the middle of an asthma attack because they knew the tenser I was, the more difficult it was to inhale the oxygen I desperately needed. Relaxing when you're in the middle of fighting for your life doesn't make sense. But, the fact is, it's the way to more oxygen. I think trusting in God and His plan in the midst of utter agony mostly doesn't make sense but, the fact is, it's the only way to peace. The more we fight and raise our fist, the more distraught and lost we become.

I think why Mike felt calm when he prayed in the face of Wendy's death was because God drew near to Him. And when the God of the universe draws near to you, you change. Your situation may stay the same or even get worse, but when His hand touches your heart and soul, something unexplainable happens.

I think it's like relaxing in the middle of an asthma attack. Breathing becomes a little easier.

Reflections

♦ Is God really good? The Bible says God is good (Mark 10:18), but our experience in life is often at odds with this assertion. With pain, suffering, and disorder all around us, how do we know He is good? Reflect on this. What is your answer?

1. we trust & believe by faith
2. we see his goodness — vs. distructive pain etc caused by Evil

♦ How have you experienced God's goodness? Are your experiences more about circumstances, or are they about how you have experienced God relationally?

When I'm in the midst of a struggle - he comforts, encourages, lifts - but he doesn't take the struggle away. He reminds me this world is not my home - it's my training ground

♦ If circumstances are not a barometer of God's goodness, then what is? How do you experience God's goodness?

His omnipotence
his nearness
" encouragement through the word & others

- Are you a person who likes to be in control? Have you had an experience where you were completely out of control? How did you feel? What did you do?

  very scary but caused me to F.R.O.G. and the push to do that is awesome even in the scaryness.

- Which part of Mike's story spoke to you the most? How so?

. . . .

God is good. Trust in Him.

10

God can use you. Serve Him.

"Take away the stone," he said.

JOHN 11:39

We all have issues, right? We all have stuff in our lives that keeps us from fully entering into all that God has planned for us. Tom, a retired African-American police officer, has a name for these issues. He calls them "stones," an analogy that comes from the story of Lazarus (John 11:38–44). Tom compares the stone in front of Lazarus's grave, which kept him from the living, to stones in our lives that keep us from fully living.

Tom personally knows all about stones. Born in North Carolina in 1939, he was one of seventeen children. His father was an alcoholic and his mother did farmwork, getting paid in peas, beans, and old clothes. Tom dropped out of high school in the tenth grade and struggled as a young man with issues of self-worth and depression.

Two men changed his young life. First was a Jewish man named Gilbert Paisner. When Tom was in his late teens, he moved to New

York City at the invitation of some friends. He walked the city streets for weeks looking for a job when Gilbert took an interest in him, finally giving him work and a place to live. Gilbert invested time in Tom, teaching him to think through the moral ramifications of his decisions and actions.

The second man who impacted Tom was a priest. While in New York, Tom struggled with feeling like his life had no purpose. He felt lost and despondent. One afternoon as he walked down the street with tears rolling down his cheeks, he decided to go into a church. The priest inside the church took the time to talk with Tom. He told Tom, "God loves you very much, and you don't need me to talk to God for you. God wants you to come to Him yourself. I want you to go home, kneel by your bed, and talk to God just like you're talking to me." Tom did what the priest told him, and as he knelt and poured out his heart to the Lord, he felt the presence of God fill the room. His whole body experienced a sort of searing sensation, and from that day forward, Tom was a different man.

These two men were stone-rollers in Tom's life, opening doors that helped him step into the future that God had planned for him. Tom's life story evolved into rolling stones for other people, and it was a vision he ignited in his community.

. . . .

Tom leaned against the dingy wall and swallowed hard, trying to push down his emotions. "Lord, I promise You if I can get to retirement, I'll try to make a difference in these kids' lives," he whispered. Hearing footsteps behind him, he quickly brushed away the tears.

"Hi, Tom," a chipper voice called out.

Turning toward the voice, Tom forced a smile. "Hi, Ms. Lawrence. How are you this afternoon?"

"Good. How are you?"

"Just fine," Tom fibbed. "On to my next classroom."

Walking down the hallway, Tom's throat grew tight as he thought about how much he loved these children. They were little sponges, waiting to soak up life. And, after walking the streets for years as a patrol officer in inner-city, drug-infested neighborhoods, he appreciated his new school assignment. Yet this work toyed more with his emotions. Every time he looked into the children's faces, he saw himself—a poverty-stricken, insecure little boy with little chance for a bright future. Many of the children he taught came from struggling inner-city homes with at least one alcoholic or drug-addicted parent. They came to school dirty, hungry, and some without a coat on the coldest of winter days.

As Tom stepped into the next third grade classroom, the children erupted. "Officer Friendly!" they shouted. They quickly forgot the math lesson they'd been doing as they clambered toward him. They held his hands, hugged his legs, and tugged on his starched uniform. The twentysomething schoolteacher clapped her hands and shouted, "Children, back to your seats!" But no one seemed to hear.

In a booming voice Tom commanded, "Now you all sit back down and listen to your teacher!" His words were firm but a smile edged up his face. The children scrambled back to their desks, and he seized the opportunity to launch into the month's value-based lesson.

"Now I have a question for you. Why do we have rules? Why is obeying your teacher and obeying school rules so important?" Tom walked to the chalkboard and picked up a piece of white chalk. On the board he wrote, "Why have rules?" underlining the word *rules*.

When he turned around, a dozen little hands were waving frantically. Tom savored their sweet enthusiasm. One boy in the front row was nearly lifting off his seat as his hand waved back and forth. "Yes?" Tom pointed at the boy. "What's your name?"

"Henry." His little face burst into a smile, revealing two missing front teeth. Henry's filthy shirt was on backward and his tennis shoes

didn't match. Tom noticed one shoe seemed much larger than the other.

"Henry, what do you think?"

"Because if we don't do what Miss Lindsay says, we ain't allowed to go to the playground and we got to stay in here and clean the boards."

"That's right," Tom agreed, walking over to Henry. He placed his hand on the boy's shoulder. "Henry makes a good point. There are consequences when we don't obey rules." His voice was gentle yet thick with authority. "Who can tell me what the word *consequence* means?"

Tom saw a girl in the back row raise her arm halfway, then put it back down. Her hair was a mess of matted cornrows, and her blue dress was threadbare. When she saw Tom looking at her, she quickly glanced down at her desk.

Tom walked over to her and tenderly asked, "What's your name, young lady?"

"Selma." Her big brown eyes framed with long thick eyelashes looked up at him.

"Selma, I bet you know what the word *consequence* means."

She nodded. "You get something taken away."

Tom nodded at her approvingly, and a shy smile crept up Selma's face, showing off adorable dimples in each of her round cheeks.

"Did you all hear what Selma said?" Tom turned and walked to the front of the room. "There are consequences when we don't obey the rules. That means something negative happens to us." Going back to the board, he wrote the word *consequence*.

"This is a big word. But you all are big children and need to under-stand this word." Walking back and forth in front of the classroom, he continued. "Rules are set up by your school and by our city to help keep people safe. Your mommy and daddy also set up rules to keep you safe."

"My daddy's in jail," one boy blurted out.

"I don't have no daddy," another boy said.

Pretty soon a dozen little mouths were all chirping at once. Tom raised his hands and the children were quiet. But Henry, once again, was waving his hand wildly, looking as if he might explode. "Yes, Henry?" Tom couldn't resist the boy.

"My daddy left my mama and I was wondering, Officer Friendly, if you could be my new daddy?"

"Me too! Be my daddy too!" another child hollered.

A lightning bolt of emotion struck Tom's heart. He looked at Henry and saw the shimmer of hope in his innocent, clear eyes. A slow smile gathered up Tom's cheeks. "You know what, Henry?"

"What, Officer Friendly?"

"You all are my children." He opened out his arms wide and the children cheered. "That's right. All of you are my children!"

Tom worked as Officer Friendly with the inner-city schools of Washington, D.C., for eighteen years before his retirement. Committed to keeping the promise he'd made to the Lord, he asked God what He wanted him to do in his retirement. One Sunday morning as he was kneeling during church, praying, he saw himself sitting behind a desk inside an old two-bedroom rental house he'd bought for investment purposes. In his mind's eye he saw a woman bringing children to him as he sat at the desk.

After the church service, he looked at his wife, Lucille, and announced, "I'm not going to sell that rental house on Wylie Street!"

"Really?" She raised her eyebrows.

"I'm going to open it as a Family Service Center!"

"What's a Family Service Center?" Lucille's eyebrows raised a notch higher.

"I don't know, but we'll find out!" He laughed, wrapping up his wife in a hug.

As Tom got the house ready to open, he asked God to give the center a name. One afternoon he sat on the cement steps in front of the house with his elbows on his knees and his chin cupped in his hands.

His thoughts drifted to his childhood when he would sit for hours on the banks of a river near his home in North Carolina. He remembered how everyone around him would be catching fish but no matter how long and hard he tried, he never caught much of anything. There were always bubbles dancing on the water around his fishing line, but never any fish. Tom's thoughts then shifted to how Jesus told His disciples, "Come, follow me . . . I will make you fishers of men" (Matt. 4:19).

A car drove by with blaring music but Tom barely noticed it. *Lord* . . . He lifted his chin out of his hands. *My life is like those bubbles on top of the water. Without You, I won't be catching anything.* A shiver ran though him. *That's the name, isn't it, Lord? The Fishing School.*

A few weeks later Tom opened the doors to the Fishing School. Not really sure how the whole vision was going to unfold, he sat on the front porch steps once again with his hands under his chin. *Lord, how are we going to get kids here now?* As he sat mulling it over, five young girls walked down the street. When a group of boys drove by, the girls shook their bodies in provocative moves. The boys called out lewd comments as they passed. When the car was out of sight, the girls turned their attention to Tom. "Hey Mister, whacha doin'? Whacha got in that house?"

Tom perked up. "I've got a Fishing School."

"What? You got fish in there? Can we come see?"

"Sure!" Tom jumped up and opened the front door.

As the girls piled into the house, they asked Tom again, "Whacha doin' in this house?"

"I'm teaching young people just like you."

"Can you teach me how to be a cosmetologist?" inquired one girl wearing a bright pink top.

"Before you can learn to be a cosmetologist, you have to learn self-respect."

"Whachu talkin' 'bout?" Brimming with teenage attitude, the girl crossed her arms.

Tom grabbed the moment. "Come in here." He led them into a room with a large rectangular table. "Have a seat and I'll explain." The girls eagerly pulled out chairs and sat down.

"Other people will treat you like you treat yourself." He looked around the table into the eyes of each girl. "You need to respect yourself in order to be treated with respect."

"I respect myself!" one of the girls, wearing a low-cut T-shirt, protested.

"When you shake your bodies at boys or wear clothes that are revealing, you're sending a message to others."

"What message?"

"The message that you're an object not to be regarded with respect. But do you know what the Bible says about you?"

They shook their heads.

"You are God's children. You are made in His image. Do you know what that means?"

Again, they all shook their heads.

"That means you deserve respect!"

For the next hour, Tom and the girls talked. They quickly opened up to him, sharing some of their struggles and aspirations. He invited them to come back the next afternoon so they could talk more.

Since that first afternoon in March of 1990, the Fishing School has offered thousands of children in D.C. a safe haven where they can get off the streets after school. It's a place where children are loved in the name of Christ by volunteers and given help to roll away any "stones" that may hinder them from living the life that God has for them.

Tom often gets the opportunity to share the story behind the Fishing School, and he always says, "We are stone-rollers at the Fishing School. All around us are crack neighborhoods, and people who are walking around like they're half dead. They're not living the life God intended. We're doing what Jesus told us to do, 'Take away the stone and take off the grave clothes.'"

Tom loves ending his Fishing School story with one question: "Who has rolled away your stones?"

. . . .

Sandee. Ray. Bertha. Debbie. These are just a few of my stone-rollers—people who have helped remove obstacles so I can grow closer to God and step more inside the life He designed for me.

Jesus could have chosen any number of ways for the Lazarus story to unfold, but what is so remarkable is that He enlists those who are with Him to remove the stone and unbind Lazarus. It amazes me to think that God asks us to participate with Him in what He is doing. But He does! Picture yourself as part of the Lazarus resurrection scene described in John 11:38–44:

A deeply emotional Jesus comes to the cave where Lazarus was buried. You are standing and talking with a small group of friends when Jesus looks over at you and says, "Take away the stone."

What?! That's crazy! You look at your friends to see if they're thinking the same thing.

"But there will be a terrible stench!" Lazarus's sister Martha blurts out, saving you from having to say what you're thinking.

Jesus reaches out and puts His hand on Martha's arm. "Didn't I tell you that if you believed, you would see the glory of God?"

Jesus looks again at you and your friends and nods. Although you are still hesitant, you walk over to the stone with your friends and start to push. A surge of adrenaline rushes through you and the stone starts to move. You brace yourself for the stench. But when the stone is no longer sealing the grave, you realize you don't smell much of anything.

Jesus calls in a loud voice, "Lazarus, come out!"

Breathless, you watch as a dead man comes out of the tomb and stands right next to you. His hands and feet are wrapped with strips of linen, and a cloth is wrapped around his face.

Jesus says to you, "Take off the grave clothes and let him go."

With shaking hands, you kneel down and begin unwrapping Lazarus's legs. Someone else kneels next to you and helps. Another person starts unbinding Lazarus's arms. It's another group effort. This is a picture of Christ calling us to work together to be His hands and feet.

Good friends of mine experienced a dog crisis that illustrates how important it is for us *all* to be participating. Here's the story as my dog-loving friend Carol relays it:

> Suzi, Nancy, Terry, and I were sitting on Suzi's porch, praying one morning. It was a beautiful spring day, and Suzi had made these spritzer juice drinks with floating strawberries. Toward the end of our prayer time, we heard a huge dogfight break out. Terry had brought her Bernese mountain dog, Mac, over to Suzi's so he could play with Suzi's young Labrador retriever, Duke. When we first heard the dogfight, Terry and Suzie jumped up and ran around the house to the back yard. Nancy and I got up a little more slowly and went through the house to join them. The dogs were entangled, and at first it was hard to tell what was going on. Both Suzi and Terry were trying to pull their dogs off and were bitten in the process. After a moment we could see that Duke's tooth was caught in Mac's collar. Both dogs were freaking out, and Suzi and Terry did everything they could to calm their dogs. We tried desperately to get the collar off Mac but couldn't, and it became obvious that he was asphyxiating. We screamed for Suzi's husband, Gil, to come help. He ran outside and worked frantically to get the collar off. After a few minutes of struggling, he was finally able to unfasten it.
>
> But it was too late. Mac was dead. "He's not breathing!"

Terry cried. Gil bolted inside to call the emergency vet. Nancy, kneeling next to the dog, placed her hand on his chest. "His heart isn't beating."

Without really thinking about it, I stuck the dog's now blue tongue back in his mouth and closed his big jaw with my hands. Years ago I had watched a program on television on how to give a dog CPR, and it all came flooding back to me as I began breathing into the dog's nose. Between breaths I told Nancy how to rhythmically push on his chest. Several long minutes passed, then Nancy exclaimed, "There's a heartbeat!" I leaned my head to his mouth but could tell he still wasn't breathing, so I kept blowing air from my lungs into the dog's nose. A few minutes later, Mac's limp tail made a single thump onto the grass. We all watched in grateful awe as Mac rejoined the living.

The thing that we talked about afterward was that if any one of us hadn't been there, Mac would have died. We needed each person there. Each person had a specific part in saving Mac's life.

This is a wild story about the cooperative efforts of my friends to save the life of a dog, but it's also a vivid picture of how we are *all* needed. Like California redwood trees that grow only in groves so that their shallow roots can intertwine and keep the massive trees from falling in the wind, we need one another. There are hurting and broken people all around us who need CPR. As my friend Mel says, "There's work to be done!" Each one of us is desperately needed. Just like Jesus enlisted the people in front of Lazarus's grave, God enlists us—to roll stones, reach out to the walking dead, and unbind them.

> Each one should use whatever gift he has
> received to serve others, faithfully administering
> God's grace in its various forms.
> 1 PETER 4:10

For many of us, this is a dare we do not take. We get stuck in the messes of our own lives. We focus inward and stagnate. We have excuses, and usually they're pretty good ones. Yet what we miss is that stone-rolling not only unbinds those we reach out to, it unbinds *us*. Picture yourself back in Lazarus's story, helping roll away the stone. Can you imagine the impact on your own life? Your own faith? Can you hear your dinner conversation that night with your family and friends as you tell them all what happened? And to think, you were part of it!

As stone-rollers, we participate in the power of God and become more alive. We taste a fresh joy as we watch others come to life. Our hearts are invigorated with purpose and passion and our faith is bolstered.

So let's live a little . . . and take the dare Tom took . . . and become stone-rollers.

Reflections

♦ Who are some of the stone-rollers in your life? What stones have they rolled away?

Stone-roller: _____ Stone: _____

Stone-roller: _____ Stone: _____

Truth Dare

Stone-roller: _____ Stone: _____

Stone-roller: _____ Stone: _____

♦ Some stone-rollers help remove physical barriers such as poverty or hunger; some stone-rollers educate and equip; some stone-rollers make an investment of time, uncovering the God-imbued value of another person. What are other things stone-rollers might do?

_____

_____

_____

_____

_____

_____

_____

♦ What are some of the most common excuses you use to not reach out to others, or to stay uninvolved in ministry?

_time_____

_____

_____

_____

_____

_____

_____

♦ Who in your life needs hope? How might you be able to reach out to this person?

_____

_____

_____

_____

_____

_____

_____

_____

♦ Which part of Tom's story spoke to you the most? How so?

_____

_____

_____

_____

_____

God can use you. Serve Him.

Conclusion

I hope that, like me, the stories in this book have rubbed into you and opened up new places for you to go with God, new terrain to trust Him in, new ways to go "farther up and further in" in your faith. If you are reading this book and found yourself wanting to know God for the first time in a deep and personal way—like the men and women in these stories knew Him—be assured He is *passionate about you*. He loves you fiercely regardless of your past or your struggles right now. We *all* fall short and fail in life—every last one of us. Yet through Christ we can be set right with God. Anyone who believes and accepts that Jesus was and is who He claimed to be is restored back to the place God always wanted us to be—with Him forever and ever. Jesus says to you and I, "I am the way and the truth and the life. No one comes to the Father except through me" (John 14:6).

The most important dare we can take in this life is to believe God—to really, truly believe Him—and then allow our lives to be swept up in the current of His truth. Once we yield ourselves to His truth, the axes of our lives change and we become different people. We operate from a different paradigm than the world. It's a place of hope and infinite possibilities, a place of trust and letting go, a place of remembrance and expectance.

It is a place of truth . . . and dare.